Family Strategies

Family
Strategies

This workbook consists of five sections with thirty-seven modules for structured interventions, pertinent didactic, and reproducible handouts.

This workbook is one of four tools for professionals.
>   Anger Strategies
>   Depression Strategies
>   Family Strategies
>   Relapse Toolkit Strategies

Claudia Black

CENTRAL RECOVERY PRESS

LAS VEGAS

Central Recovery Press (CRP) is committed to publishing exceptional materials addressing addiction treatment, recovery, and behavioral healthcare topics.

For more information, visit www.centralrecoverypress.com.

Publisher: Central Recovery Press
3321 N. Buffalo Drive
Las Vegas, NV 89129

24 23 22 21 20 19   1 2 3 4 5

ISBN: 978-1-942094-92-0 (paper)
978-1-942094-93-7 (e-book)

Photo of Claudia Black by Winifred Whitfield. Used with permission.

Every attempt has been made to contact copyright holders. If copyright holders have not been properly acknowledged please contact us. Central Recovery Press will be happy to rectify the omission in future printings of this book.

Cover design and interior by Deb Tremper, Six Penny Graphics

Special Thanks

To Sandi Klein, my assistant for many years, who once again has been invaluable in embracing this project as it if were her own. She skillfully works with every aspect from writing, to organizing, editing, proofing, and coordinating with the many parties involved.

To Jeri Nilsen, for her many gifts as editor.

To Martha Heier, who with talent and enthusiasm readily became a team player welcoming the cover design and production work.

And to Jack Fahey, my husband and colleague, who continues to be my best friend and loyal supporter.

Together we have been a great team.

Note from Claudia Black *(First Edition)*

Addiction passes through families generationally, and is said to be the "gift that goes on giving." The use of *Family Strategies* is an opportunity for the gift to become that of recovery, the possibility of changing the individual, the immediate family, and the intergenerational transmission of addictive disorders. Change begins with one person. From a systematic viewpoint, when one person changes the way he or she functions within the family system, that system will change. This is readily evident when addiction enters a family system, and it is just as apparent when recovery enters that system.

In a therapeutic setting it is easy for the practitioner, the addicted person, and the family to view the addicted person as the identified client. *Family Strategies* facilitates shifting perspective to the family members as clients. Giving principal consideration to the family system allows everyone in the family the opportunity to develop and grow creating the potential to break the cycle of addiction.

The strategies presented in this book are those proven most effective in primary family systems therapy when addiction is either still active or the addicted person is in early recovery, regardless of the type of addiction, whether it is substance addiction, behavior, or process addiction.

This book is intended for use by clinicians, addiction counselors, and mental healthcare practitioners who are already skilled in understanding addictive disorders and their impact on families, and those who work with a family member or members in a relationship with someone actively in addiction or in recovery. It is used quite effectively with spouses, partners, parents, and adolescent or adult age children. In many sessions it is appropriate to include the addicted person, but that is at the facilitator's discretion.

In many of the strategies sections, ideas and formats are presented for structured interventions. The use of handouts in the form of written exercises, checklists, sentence stems, structured dialogues and/or art activities is an integral part of this therapeutic technique. All handouts are designed for clinicians to reproduce and use without restriction as to copyright permission.

Realizing I cannot possibly consider all of the ethnic, cultural, and educational differences a clinician may be confronted with, I trust that your sound clinical judgment will figure in the timing and delivery of these strategies. I encourage you to modify or customize them in any manner that promotes more effective use of this guide with clients.

Note from Claudia Black (*Second Edition*)

The most critical change in the world of addiction since the initial publication of *Family Strategies* is due to the abuse of opiates. As a consequence, families are confronted with faster progression of the disease on the part of the addict, and often the addict is near death or has died before the family recognizes the reality of the situation. In addition, process addictions, particularly gaming and sex addiction, are on the rise as technology fuels easy access and escalation. This makes the need for family intervention even more critical.

As stated in the first edition, my philosophy is that the family is the client, and the family includes the addicted person. Everyone in the family is struggling. Family members are often experiencing their own addiction; and their depression and anxiety are often rooted in the trauma of living with addiction. Their codependency has often preceded any adult relationships and enables the current dysfunction of the family.

Choices and opportunities for recovery occur when family members start to recognize their role in the unhealthy family system. As they step out of denial they come to recognize where their power lies and begin to take responsibility for self. Letting go of the need for approval and fears of abandonment allow them to find the willingness to set healthy boundaries and to no longer engage in enabling behaviors. Finding emotional clarity allows family members to recognize their own needs, which in turn helps to develop a stronger sense of self. Intuitively, they will find letting go of control opens space for having faith in something outside of self, allowing a relationship with a Higher Power to begin. Everyone needs to take responsibility for their part of the unhealthy couple-ship or family system. *Family Strategies* offers a wide range of exercises that create this foundation.

It takes just one person in the system to begin the cycle of change. As addiction repeats itself in families, so does recovery.

Table of Contents

Instructions

Outline of *Family Strategies*

The following is an outline of a time-limited, structured psychoeducational therapy process focusing on family recovery. While it is presented with a group orientation, it can also be used effectively with an individual participant. Read through all of the sessions and become familiar with the content so you will be able to be flexible as needed. You know the needs of your participants better than the author. You may want to use all of the sessions in the sequence presented, or you may simply pick and choose those that are most relevant to your participants.

You are encouraged to be creative and bring your own style of work into this process. Remember, this outline is meant only to be a guide.

Suggested Time

Time required depends on whether or not this guide is used with an individual, or in a group setting. Sessions can be condensed or expanded by use of opening and closing rituals, time offered to complete exercises, and depth of discussion. Know how much time you want to give the opening and closing rituals so that you will easily transition to the focus of the particular session. While most sessions for a group take one and one half hours, they could be expanded to a lengthier format, or condensed for an individual.

Suggested Opening of Each Session

Sessions are to begin and end on time with a ritual opening and closing of each session. The author suggests the sessions open with one of the following possibilities:

- A centering technique such as a relaxation exercise;
- A centering check-in, where each participant shares with one or two words what they are experiencing physically (e.g., tired, energetic), emotionally (e.g., frustrated, lonely), and spiritually (e.g., apart from, in tune with, at peace, disconnected);

- A review of the last session by the facilitator, followed by each participant responding by identifying what they valued most from the previous session;
- A question or comment period about the previous session;
- Reading from a daily self-help meditation book.

Confidentiality

Consult your state regulations; the most common exceptions regard suicide, homicide, and child and elder abuse. If working with an individual or family, explain your professional and/or agency's parameters of confidentiality at time of initial meeting. If working with a group, each session needs to begin with a statement of confidentiality. Suggested form: a pledge that each individual makes. "I pledge what I see, do, and hear here will stay here." The facilitator should expand on that statement as required by state and federal regulations, such as adding, *except in the interest of your treatment with other treatment team members and in regard to state and federal regulations.*

Didactic

Didactic refers to educational information that you may offer in a lecture-type format. This is information you are welcome to use verbatim or as a model to improvise upon. Sessions that include such information are indicated by the word *Didactic.* To signify that the didactic portion has come to a close, this icon will be used:

 Didactic closed

When the didactic is resumed, the inverse of this icon will so indicate.

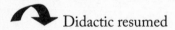 Didactic resumed

Handouts

Handouts are included and are a part of most sessions. You may reproduce them without restriction as to copyright permission. Many of the handouts are best completed and discussed during the course of a particular session, while others may be given as an assignment.

Assignments

Depending upon the motivation of the participants and the session length, assignments relevant to the focus on recovery are often an expedient use of their time. Prior to offering an assignment, garner their commitment to follow through. Be clear with instructions and expectations. Always follow up on the assignment in the subsequent session. When a participant chooses not to do an assignment, consider the following:

1. Spend some time in the session doing an assignment that was unfinished.
2. Evaluate your initial rationale and explanation of the tasks; e.g., "Did I make the task(s) clear, simple, and linked to some payoff/benefit; or, did the participant perceive it as busy work?"
3. Evaluate the appropriate fit between the task assigned and the participant's ability to perform it; e.g., is the unmet assignment related to participant's inability to perform it or unwillingness to comply? Could you facilitate the success by breaking assignments down into smaller, more easily performable pieces?
4. Encourage participant to observe, day-by-day, her/his skillful efforts to avoid, resist, and deceive their self with reasons to fail. Make them expert observers of self-sabotage.
5. Examine precisely all decisions that the participant made during the interval between sessions to avoid follow through, and label them "decisions," "choices."

Guided Imageries

There are several sessions that include the opportunity for a guided imagery. The imageries are written out for the facilitator to present. With the exception of the Closure Imagery, all other imageries can be downloaded from CRP's website if the presenter prefers to offer a pre-recorded version.

- Letting Go of Control Imagery (Section Two – Session Four)
- Letting Go of the Pain of Grief Imagery (Section Four – Session Seven)
- Letting Go of Resentments Imagery (Section Four – Session Six)
- Connecting to a Higher Power Imagery (Section Five – Session Two)
- Letting Go of Secrets Imagery (Section Three – Session Seven)
- Affirmation Imagery (Section Four – Session Eight)
- Closure Imagery

Suggested Closing of Each Session

Ask participants to respond to one of the following remarks:

- I learned that ...
- I was surprised that ...
- I remembered that ...
- What I would like to learn more about is ...
- What I did not understand was ...

Asking the participants to make these statements further validates their participation and experience. It is also helpful for you to hear what they prioritize in terms of their learning experience.

Twelve-Step Resources

Twelve-step programs are a valuable resource for participants and they are found in most communities throughout the United States. You are encouraged to familiarize yourself with those located in your area. Al-Anon meetings are for family and friends of the alcoholic, drug addict, or other substance abuser. In some communities there are similar programs for the family of sex addicts—CoSA, or for gambling addicts—Gam-Anon—and ACA (Adult Children of Alcoholics) meetings, which are no longer specific just to alcoholic families but are open to anyone who identifies with being raised in a dysfunctional family system. And, in some communities, there are Co-Dependents Anonymous meetings—CoDA.

Viewing the Family Addiction

Overview

This section offers family members the opportunity to dialogue and explore how the family is a part of the addicted system. The predominant theme is that addiction does not just impact the addicted person, but belongs to the entire family. The family, including the addict, will be able to recognize codependency as its own addictive process and how addiction and codependency are multigenerational. This begins the process of recognizing the social and emotional impact of addiction on their own family and offers an opportunity for honest dialogue with each other.

Codependency as an Addiction offers family members the opportunity to realize they have their own issues from which to recover, and their behavior is quite similar to that of the addicted person.

Sharing the Disease is a structured dialogue that facilitates sharing between family members. It can only be meaningful after education about addiction and co-addiction.

Family Tree is an extremely helpful tool for the family to recognize generational patterns and influences. It takes the blame away from any one person and helps the family to realize the gravity and extensiveness of addiction and its many complexities.

Family Diagram offers the family a visual portrait of the centrality of addiction and the connectedness of the different family members.

Assumptions begins a dialogue between the addict and family members that clarifies misperceptions and enhances communication. This exercise can be planned later in the treatment process, but using it as the family begins recovery sets the tone between all of the family members that they are ready for honesty and directness.

Addictive Behaviors may or may not be appropriate at this beginning stage of the treatment process, but the facilitator needs to be prepared to introduce the idea of addictive behaviors spontaneously to family members of the identified addicted person.

Codependency as an Addiction

Family Objectives

To recognize codependency as an addictive disorder.

To identify addictive symptoms, behaviors, and feelings.

Materials Needed

Handout – My Symptoms, Behaviors, Feelings

Handout – Addiction Symptoms, Behaviors, Feelings

Starting Point

The word *codependency* has been used as a noun, verb, and adjective for several decades. It has been used so freely it can trivialize the seriousness of a family member's despair and self-destructive coping behaviors. The reality is codependency fuels depression, anxiety disorders, unhealthy parenting, severe relational difficulties, and suicide.

While codependency is not a formal clinical diagnosis, it has been a helpful framework in language for the layperson to both understand his or her behavior and thinking and forge a path to healing and recovery.

Codependency is a set of self-defeating beliefs and behaviors stemming from internalized toxic shame with its roots frequently coming from childhood developmental trauma. It is most often reflected in the person who has not developed a strong sense of self, is unable to maintain healthy boundaries, and finds their identity based on their relationships with others.

The purpose of this session is for family members to recognize how their self-defeating behaviors are frequently the same behaviors, feelings, and thought processes that are a part of an addictive process. The behavior of the addicted person and his or her loved one is often a shared disease.

This can be presented in two manners: 1) If family members are new to education about addiction, review the information on the handout in the columns describing Symptoms, Behaviors, and Feelings, focusing on the addict's experience. Then go back through the Symptoms, Behaviors, and Feelings focusing on the codependent family member's experiences. This can be an interactive discussion by relying on participants to give examples and using the handout *My Symptoms, Behaviors, Feelings*; 2) If family members are familiar with the disease model of addiction having had previous treatment experience, then review the Symptoms, Behaviors, and Feelings alternating examples of the addict and the codependent.

The following examples are helpful for the facilitator's knowledge, but can also be presented in didactic form.

Didactic

Disease Symptoms

Preoccupation—the addict has a repetitive focus on behaviors connected to his/her acting out behavior; the codependent experiences the inability to focus on other things without intrusive thoughts about the addicted person and his/her behaviors.

> *Addict:* "I wonder if there's enough booze at home or if my dealer will be home or if I have enough money for my drugs." "I will need to cover my bases with my family by . . ."

> *Codependent:* "I wonder where my husband is, who he is with, and what I will say to him when he gets home."

Increased Tolerance—the addict needs to engage more frequently in the behavior or with the substance to garner the desired affect, which is usually related to a neurochemical change; the codependent displays a willingness to accept inappropriate and/or hurtful behavior with lower expectation, which is usually related to a psychological tolerance.

Addict: "I used to get drunk on six beers. Now it takes me a dozen." "I used to be satisfied with pornographic magazines, now I need contact with someone on the internet who will interact with me."

Codependent: "He used to be critical of me and I would get really upset; now he calls me horrible names and it's no big deal to me."

Loss of Control—the addict is no longer able to predict engaging or using behavior; the codependent is also no longer able to predict his/her own behavior.

Addict: "I told myself I was only going to spend fifty dollars at the casino and lost my whole paycheck before I left." "I told myself I would only have one glass of wine at the wedding and I got drunk and passed out."

Codependent: "When I know that he is going to be late for dinner again, my plan is to give him the cold shoulder and go about my business. On occasion I'll snap. Yesterday I planned on ignoring him but I ended up screaming in front of the kids. I, not my husband, was out of control."

Denial—the addict and codependent erect defenses to rationalize and minimize thereby supporting the behavior.

Addict: "My children have not been affected by my drinking." "Everybody drinks, don't they? It doesn't mean I'm alcoholic."

Codependent: "There's nothing wrong with me. He has the problem, not me. I don't need to change." "The kids have not been affected by me or my behavior."

Blackouts—blackouts are the one symptom the addict experiences that is not an exact carryover to the codependent. The substance addict has a period of amnesia, usually lasting from hours to days. He or she is conscious and interacting, but the memory is not imprinted on the brain, and therefore it cannot be recalled. The codependent's blackout, often referred to as a 'brown-out,' is due to the stress of heightened emotions; there is too much emotionally charged stimuli for details of what occurred to be recorded. It may not be as well-delineated a block of memory as a substance abuse blackout. It is more a sense of something occurring without clarity. This could be referred to as a trance-like or dissociative experience in which the memory may or may not be recorded and not readily available for conscious memory. The blackout of the process addict—i.e. gambler, sex addict—is more similar to the codependent's than the substance abuser's.

Addict: "I don't know where I was, what I did, or who I was with last night."

Codependent: "We had a screaming fight the other night. I don't remember exactly what I said."

Craving—the addict has a severe physical or psychological urge or craving to reengage in the substance or behavior; the codependent experiences a deep obsessive psychological urge or longing for the times when things were better. Frequently craving goes hand in hand with euphoric recall (romanticizing the good times).

Addict: "I wanted cocaine so bad I could taste it."

Codependent: "I really miss him. When he is gone I ache for him."

Compulsive Behavior—addicts begin engaging in behavior in a manner that they feel is driven, obsessed, and they do so repeatedly, which often reduces cravings or preoccupation; codependents may begin engaging in behaviors such as snooping, spending, eating, sex, etc. Codependents' compulsivity may be acted out in perfectionist tendencies.

Addict: "When I had a craving, I knew I shouldn't drink, but I found myself in the bar last night anyway."

Codependent: "My house is clean with everything in its place. It makes up for how I feel inside."

Decreased Tolerance—progressively the addict cannot engage or use to the extent he or she once did and begins to experience negative symptoms more quickly; the codependent becomes less patient and is less likely to stay in denial and may experience an emotional bottom. (Usually these symptoms transpire more in the latter stages of the addictive process.)

Addict: "I used to be able to stay out for hours using, and now I am in trouble shortly after I begin."

Codependent: "I can't take any more. Everything he does irritates me."

Medical Problems—

Addict: In the latter stages of addiction, particularly if the addict is a substance abuser, physical problems can run the gamut from heart and lung disease, brain disease, liver damage, throat and mouth diseases, to diabetes and digestive disorders.

Medical problems may also be related to unsafe sexual practices, accidents, and injury.

Codependent: More apt to experience stress-related health problems such as headaches, stomach or digestive problems, hives, back problems, ulcers, depression and/or anxiety; many diseases codependents suffer are fueled and complicated by stress—most specifically, autoimmune disorders.

Disease Behaviors

Moving on to the Behavior column, continue the discussion on the handout by having participants identify the ways they rationalized, minimized, and blamed. They can identify sneaking, lying, hiding and secrets, and how they isolated. They can also identify with euphoric recall, which is focusing on the good times or the good qualities of the addict, to the exclusion of the more painful times. Euphoric recall can take the form of tunnel vision—a myopic, biased, and unrealistic portrait of the addict's behavior that helps to maintain denial.

Feelings

Frozen or *numb feelings* refers to the inability to experience feelings, feeling disconnected from one's emotional self. While family members may readily grasp the concept of frozen or numb feelings, it is often a new description to them. If they identify with feeling frozen or numb during this discussion, ask them to circle feelings they can identify with and then write two examples for each feeling they have circled. A simple shift from dialoguing to self-reflection and putting thoughts down on paper creates momentum for further awareness and then more discussion. Anger, loneliness, sadness and disappointment, guilt, fear, and shame are feelings family members are most apt to be able to identify.

To enhance discussion regarding feelings, ask participants to share examples of each feeling or describe on a scale of 1 to 10 (1 being not at all, 10 being engulfed by the feeling) how they relate.

The handout *My Symptoms, Behaviors, Feelings* can also be given as an assignment so as to give participants more time to complete and then discuss.

My Symptoms, Behaviors, Feelings

Fill in examples of your symptoms, behaviors, and feelings.

DISEASE SYMPTOMS	
Preoccupation	
Increased Tolerance	
Loss of Control	
Denial	
Blackouts	
Craving	
Compulsive Behavior	
Decreased Tolerance	
Medical Problems	

DISEASE BEHAVIORS	
Rationalizing	
Minimizing	
Blaming	
Sneaking/Lying	
Hiding/Secrets	
Isolating	
Euphoric Recall	

FEELINGS 1–10	
Frozen Feelings	
Anger	
Blaming	
Loneliness	
Sadness	
Disappointment	
Guilt	
Fear	
Shame	

Addiction Symptoms, Behaviors, Feelings

DISEASE SYMPTOMS
Preoccupation Addict: I didn't hear what she said as I was thinking about getting high. Codependent: Where is he? Who is he with?
Increased Tolerance Addict: I used to get high on a few drinks, now it takes more to feel good. Codependent: It's no big deal that he drinks.
Loss of Control Addict: I didn't plan to spend so much money. Codependent: I was going to ignore him but ended up screaming at him.
Denial Addict: I've got it under control. Codependent: He has the problem, not me.
Blackouts Addict: I have no idea who I was with last night. Codependent: We had a fight but I can't remember exactly what I said.
Craving Addict: I need it—I can feel it in my bones. Codependent: I'll take her back in any condition. I miss her so much.
Compulsive Behavior Addict: I know I shouldn't go to the bar, but I just couldn't help it. Codependent: I cleaned the whole house to make up for how I feel.
Decreased Tolerance Addict: I lose control so quickly now. Codependent: I can't stand it anymore.
Medical Problems Addict: I wouldn't be in the hospital if I hadn't been high while driving. Codependent: The doctor says I'm developing an ulcer.

DISEASE BEHAVIORS
Rationalizing Addict: I work hard. I deserve my 'high' time. Codependent: There are other kids a lot worse than him.
Minimizing Addict: But it's not this way most of the time. Codependent: It's not always this bad.
Blaming Addict: If my partner would do her part, I wouldn't have to get high. Codependent: It's his co-worker's fault he got fired.
Sneaking/Lying Addict: I have to lie to cover my losses. Codependent: I lied to his boss for him.
Hiding/Secrets Addict: My wife knows I use cocaine, but not that I gamble. Codependent: I didn't tell anyone I found her passed out on the floor.
Isolating Addict: I don't go out with my friends anymore. Codependent: I'll just stay in my room.
Euphoric Recall Addict: It's such a rush—I just want that feeling again. Codependent: I just want the man I married back.

FEELINGS
Frozen Feelings
Anger
Loneliness
Sadness
Disappointment
Guilt
Fear
Shame
Other

Sharing the Disease

Family Objectives

To develop a better understanding that addiction is a family disease.

To enhance communication.

Materials Needed

Handout – Impact of Addiction

Starting Point

This session can only be meaningful after education about addiction and codependency. It was created to involve the addict, but may be adapted for, and be of value to, a codependents-only group. When utilized with both addicts and codependent family members it can lead to a meaningful discussion that allows family members a greater understanding that addiction is a family illness. Ask participants to write out their responses to the list of questions from the appropriate column on the *Impact of Addiction* handout. When everyone has finished, have them share with family members.

If this is a large therapy group of multiple families it can be helpful for participants to partner up with a person from another family to share with that person. Example—a participant partners with an addict from another family. Listening to someone outside of one's immediate family can help the participant realize that his or her situation is not unique and aids the family in generating an understanding and empathy for the impact of the disease.

Impact of Addiction

Addict

- How long have you been addicted?
- How long have you been dealing with addiction generationally? (i.e. father was alcoholic, grandfather was workaholic, etc.)
- How and in what ways do you see your addiction progressing?
- How do you see yourself losing control over your addictive behaviors?
- What do you think is the biggest consequence that addiction and codependency has had on you and your family?
- Give two examples of defenses you've used that have kept you in denial.

Codependent

- How long have you been codependent?
- How long have you been dealing with addiction generationally? (i.e., father was alcoholic, grandmother was compulsive overeater, etc.)
- How and in what ways do you see your codependency progressing?
- How do you see yourself losing control over your behavior?
- What do you think is the biggest consequence that addiction and codependency has had on you and your family?
- Give two examples of defenses you've used that have kept you in denial.

Family Tree

Family Objective

To recognize the generational legacy of addictive disorders.

Materials Needed

Handout – Family Tree Board

Starting Point

For family members to better understand their family system, it is helpful to have a mental picture of their family. Once addiction emerges in a family, it is seldom a genetic exception or anomaly. A family tree is a valuable tool for demonstrating generational patterns and influences so that family members can recognize them. Using the handout *Family Tree* as an outline, ask participants to create their family tree and then discuss.

This is a valuable exercise that can be done in a family session allowing all family members to contribute. This would be best created on a board for all to review.

Family Tree

Diagram your family of origin back two generations. After entering each person's name, record any of the following characteristics by placing the letter(s) of the characteristic next to the name. Participant is welcome to identify and explore any additional theme in his or her family as well.

A = Alcoholic or Addict	CA = Victim of Child Abuse
G = Compulsive Gambler	CI = Chronic Illness
A/B = Anorexic/Bulimic	MH = Mental Health Disorders; Depression/Bipolar/Anxiety
O = Compulsive Overeater	OCB = Compulsive / Addictive Behavior (please label)
SA = Sex Addict	PA = Partner of Addict

If you are unsure, but have a good guess about an individual's characteristic, simply put the letter(s) of your guess and circle it. Thus, if grandfather John Smith was a compulsive overeater and you think he was an alcoholic as well, you would enter John Smith – O & A.

MOTHER'S SIDE	FATHER'S SIDE
Maternal Grandparents Grandmother/Grandfather	Paternal Grandparents Grandmother/Grandfather
_____ _____	_____ _____
Name Aunts and their Spouses	Name Aunts and their Spouses
_____	_____

Name Children   Name Children

_____   _____

_____   _____

_____   _____

_____   _____

_____   _____

_____   _____

_____   _____

_____   _____

_____   _____   _____   _____

               _____   _____

               _____   _____

               _____   _____

               _____   _____

Name Uncles and their Spouses   Name Uncles and their Spouses

_____   _____   _____   _____

               Name Children   Name Children

               _____   _____

               _____   _____

               _____   _____

               _____   _____

_____   _____   _____   _____

               _____   _____

               _____   _____

               _____   _____

               _____   _____

_____   _____   _____   _____

               _____   _____

               _____   _____

	Parents		
2nd Husband (Stepfather)	MOM	DAD	2nd Wife (Stepmother)
_____	_____	_____	_____
	_____		_____

Sisters & Brothers (Include Yourself)	Spouses	Children	
_____	_____	_____	_____
		_____	_____
_____	_____	_____	_____
		_____	_____
_____	_____	_____	_____
		_____	_____
_____	_____	_____	_____
		_____	_____
_____	_____	_____	_____
		_____	_____
_____	_____	_____	_____
		_____	

Did you discover anything new about family members while doing this exercise? If so, how does this impact you? Did seeing your family diagrammed in this way offer you any important insights? What does this family tree say to you?

_____

_____

_____

_____

Family Diagram

Family Objective

To describe their family connections.

Materials Needed

Handout – Family Diagram #1 & 2

Handout – Family Diagram #3

Handout – Family Diagram #4

Large pieces of paper and pens or pencils

Starting Point

Every family relates quite differently. This session offers an opportunity for family members to share how they see their family system. It is usually very enlightening and has great importance to the individual family members and also affords them the opportunity to identify and talk about what they would like to change within their family system and what they can do to create positive changes.

Show participants the examples given in the *Family Diagram* handouts. Diagram #1 depicts the family organized around alcohol and closed off from the outside world. Diagram #2 suggests that the gambler is isolated from other family members, but shows that they are connected and relating to each other. The gambling may be acknowledged or not, but family members have found a means to circumvent its centrality in their lives. Diagram #3 depicts a family in which the father and mother are divorced. The substance-abusing father has a "new" family. Child #2 is the contact person of the two families. It is also a prime example of the influence of extended family members. Diagram #4 depicts two addicted parents and two using children distanced from each other.

Family Strategies

Ask each family member to draw a diagram of their family system that demonstrates the predominant way in which they experience their family. Offer the *Family Diagram* handouts as examples. Remind them there is no right or wrong way to do this exercise; each person draws his or her own diagram as he or she sees it. Occasionally, someone may need to draw more than one diagram—a sober family diagram, a drinking family diagram; if the behavior is binge type, a cycle of anticipation may present as the binge approaches.

After each person has drawn a diagram of how he or she experiences the family system, display the diagrams for all participants to view. After each person has described the meaning of his/her diagram, discuss what he or she would like to change within the family system and what each one can do to make that happen.

Optional: Create a family sculpt. If the addicted person is in session, begin by having him or her physically position each person according to how he or she perceives the connectedness of the family relationships. One by one, family members then take turns repositioning (sculpting) all the other members according to how each perceives the family system. Perception of the family system is going to be different for each member, and it is important for all of them to see each other's perspective. Allow this to transition into a discussion of how they would like to see their family system work, and the changes each member will commit to for the health of a better-functioning family. If this is a multi-family group, witnessing another family's sculpt is also beneficial.

Family Diagram #1

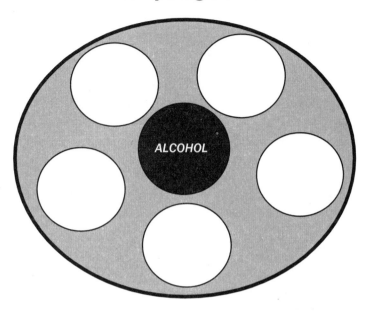

The family is organized around alcohol and closed off from the outside world.

Family Diagram #2

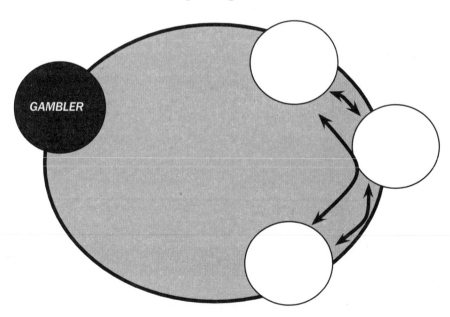

The family bypasses the gambler as a central organizing principle. The gambler is isolated from other family members, who only interact with each other. The gambling may be acknowledged or not, but family members have found a means to circumvent its centrality in their lives.

Family Diagram #3

Child #1 & #2 are close. Child #3 has relationship with Child #2 but not Child #1. Mother appears to share relationship with Child #1 & #2 but has autonomous relationship with #3. Child #3 isolates from the family, but all three children are involved in the outside world and operate outside the family. The mother does not connect with the outside world. Father (remarried) is a substance abuser and focused on his drug use. Child #2 assumes responsibility of keeping the two families in contact.

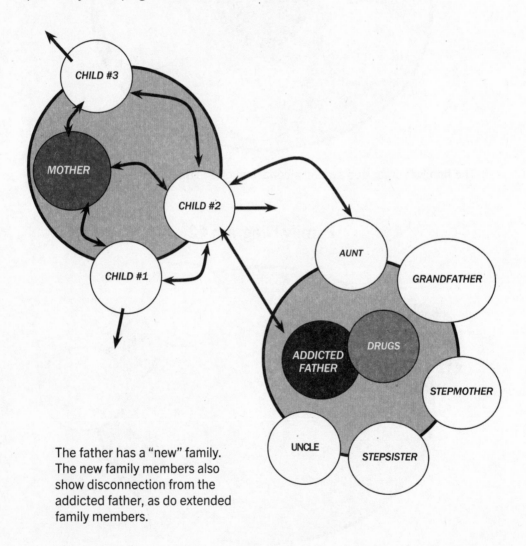

The father has a "new" family. The new family members also show disconnection from the addicted father, as do extended family members.

Family Diagram #4

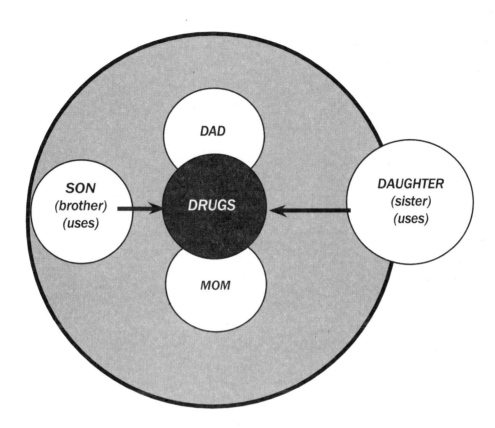

Both parents are addicted and there is little sense of family for the two children. The daughter and son are very disconnected and at opposite sides of the family circle. The brother is totally isolated from the outside world, whereas the sister connects with the outside world.

Assumptions

Family Objectives

To stop making assumptions.

To establish clear communications.

Materials Needed

Handout – Communication Exercise

Starting Point

Often problems in relationships arise because expectations are not clear, and assumptions are most likely incorrect. When communication becomes strained, many topics are avoided and secrets are kept which are very destructive to relationships. The handout *Communication Exercise* is a format that provides all family members a structure to begin healthy communication.

Statement One—In our relationship I would like from you—is answered only by family members because the addicted person could easily ask for behaviors that are inappropriate, that is, "I would like you to trust me."

The rest of the statements are directed to both the addicted person and individual family members.

Statement Two—I have assumed you knew (but in case you don't) I would like to tell you—is an opportunity to clarify a myriad of things, thus responses are often diverse. "I assumed you knew I also abused cocaine, not just alcohol." "I assumed you knew I was abused as a child." "I assumed you knew that I love you."

Statements Three and Four—These are topics I hesitate to bring up with you, I have difficulty sharing these feelings with you—offer a format to approach subjects that have been difficult to discuss. "I'm hesitant to bring up our financial situation." "I'm hesitant to talk with you about concerns I have regarding our son." "I have difficulty letting you know I'm scared." "I find it hard to tell you how much I love you." "It's hard to tell you how incredibly angry I am with you." If a participant's response indicates being afraid or angry, flush out the specific situation and behaviors that caused these feelings. It is important that one's feelings become connected to behaviors that did or did not occur.

Statements Five and Six—My use of (addictive behavior) and *your use of* (addictive behavior)—must be completed even if a participant has not previously owned up to having a problem. If there is no problem, the sentence completion will imply that. If there is a problem, that too will be implied in the responses. Sometimes, up until this point, problems have not been identified or verbalized.

Statements Seven and Eight—I feel distant from you when, I feel close to you when—allow participants to be specific about what each does to create distance and closeness. "I feel distant from you when you put down my friends." "I feel close to you when you help me with my chores."

Statement Nine—In order to improve our relationship I am willing to—offers the opportunity to identify specific behavioral changes that could be made to improve relationships and allows each participant to take responsibility for his/her part. It is important the response be specific to make the changes manageable. "In order to improve our relationship, I am willing to take time each week to sit down and listen to what's going on in your life." "In order to improve our relationship, I am willing to stop criticizing your appearance."

Statement Ten—These are the traits I value in myself—acknowledges personal positive traits and serves as an opportunity to express them. Getting recognition for things one values in oneself is an important part of relationships. Sometimes we assume that others already know what you like about yourself. "Traits I value in myself are—I'm always on time; if I say I will do something for you, I do it; my appearance is clean and neat; I am honest and trustworthy."

Statement Eleven—These are the traits I value in you—lets participants express traits they value in their family members. Just as it is assumed that someone already knows what you like about yourself, it is often assumed that it's not necessary to say positive things about someone else, believing that he or she already knows. This is generally not true in relationships involving addiction. Think about traits you value in your partner and share them. Try to focus more on who he or she is rather than on what they have done. These are things we need most to hear, yet are said the least. "I've always admired your outspoken nature and your ability to just say what you think." "You are patient and kind."

Knowing your participants, you may choose from this menu the statements that you believe would be most appropriate and helpful. Feel free to add or delete statements. This is a shared exercise between two people. One person reads all of his/her responses aloud and then the second person has a turn.

This exercise is extremely powerful and it can be tailored to any significant relationship, be it a spouse, a partner, a parent, a child, or a sibling. It is suggested the facilitator read the participants' responses before asking them to read aloud to assure that boundaries are maintained.

Communication Exercise

Complete each of the following sentences with a minimum of three statements in regard to your family member.

1. *In our relationship I would like from you*

2. *I have assumed you knew (but in case you do not), I would like to tell you*

3. *These are some topics I hesitate to bring up with you*

4. *I have difficulty sharing these feelings with you*

5. *My use of (drugs, alcohol, sex, money, etc.) has affected our relationship in these ways*

6. *Your use of (drugs, alcohol, sex, money, etc.) has affected our relationship in these ways*

7. *I feel distant from you when*

8. *I feel close to you when*

9. *In order to improve our relationship, I am willing to*

10. *These are the traits I value in myself*

11. *These are the traits I value in you*

Addictive Behaviors

Family Objective

To consider and identify whether or not family members have any addictive behaviors.

Starting Point

This session may be spontaneously incorporated at any time during the treatment process at the facilitator's discretion. If the facilitator suspects that a family member is also actively addicted, or he or she expresses concern about the possibility of addiction or addictive behavior, it is important to respond immediately. If it isn't appropriate to pursue a response in the setting in which it comes to light, set aside additional time.

It is very common to have more than one person addicted within the same family system. While the focus may be on one person, another person's addiction may not be so apparent, or as yet problematic. The addiction may be a different substance or behavior, or this other person may have such power in the family that the members are afraid to speak up. Addictive behaviors include both substance and process addictions ranging from work addiction or eating disorders to money issues, sexual acting out, gambling, compulsive spending, compulsive exercise, playing video games, or time spent on the internet.

Ask family members directly whether they believe they have any addictive behaviors.
- Are they concerned they may be drinking or engaging in some other addictive behavior excessively?
- Has anyone ever indicated to them they would like them to stop the addictive behavior?
- Would they be willing to share about their own usage and/or addictive behavior? Have they had any difficulty as a consequence of drinking or using other drugs? Have they made any efforts to decrease or stop the behavior?
- Have they been unable to maintain decreasing or stopping the behavior?

The acronym *SAFE* is a helpful way to identify or think about potential addictive or compulsive behaviors.

S	*Secretive*	Are you involved in a process or a behavior that is secretive? Is it something you do not want to talk about openly?
A	*Abusive*	Are you involved in a process or behavior that is abusive? Is it harmful or hurtful to yourself or others?
F	*Feelings*	Does this process or behavior separate or remove you from your feelings? Does it medicate your feelings? Is it the only area of your life in which you experience feelings?
E	*Emptiness*	After you have engaged in it for a while, does this process leave you with a sense of emptiness?

A discussion on addictive behaviors leads to a variety of possibilities for participants—more education about addiction and/or addictive behaviors, a referral for further help, a commitment to dialogue more about the behavior, and perhaps even an initial plan of abstinence.

Stepping Out of the Shadows

Overview

This section challenges family members to take ownership of their own lives and addresses issues that contribute to enabling behaviors and living in the shadow of the addicted person. Family members will begin to address the denial process, recognize personal behaviors that sabotage their recovery and support the active addiction, and identify the negative impact their behavior is creating. All of this helps them to take the initial steps toward the healing process.

Denial is at the heart of any addictive system. This session offers validation about the use of denial as a coping mechanism while challenging the family to be more honest.

Powerlessness and Unmanageability will bring greater meaning and understanding to family members when they realize they are not responsible for, nor able to change the addicted person's behavior. It also helps them recognize that their behavior has not helped the addict and has been hurtful to themselves.

Enabling teaches an understanding of enabling behavior and gives family members a chance to identify for themselves the behaviors they engage in that support the addiction and that sabotage recovery for themselves and the addict.

Giving Up Control is instructive for family members' appreciation that unhealthy controlling behavior is often pervasive in addictive families. Controlling behavior needs to be challenged. Letting go of some control is explored to reach acceptance of powerlessness and unmanageability. This is a foundational recovery issue meaning that without letting go of some control family members won't garner the benefit of recovery.

Powerlessness and Control will help solidify family members' recognition of powerlessness and control. Being an art exercise in and of itself is an effective tool as the very nature of using art as a medium undermines rigid controlling behavior.

Codependency First Step is meant to reinforce family members' need for recovery. Based on the First Step of Al-Anon's twelve-step self-help program for family members or significant others of the addicted person, these handouts facilitate a more in-depth explanation of a person's powerlessness and unmanageability.

Denial

Family Objectives

To recognize and further awareness of the denial process.

To understand the role of the Don't Talk Rule.

Materials Needed

Handout – Minimizing – Discounting – Rationalizing

Optional: Collage materials for each participant

3 to 5 magazines (nearly any magazine can be used; it is suggested that there be an assortment)

14" x 17" pieces of paper, scotch tape, scissors

Starting Point

In addicted family systems family members often succumb to dysfunctional family rules such as the Don't Talk Rule. While maintaining the Don't Talk Rule is not in and of itself denial, it feeds the denial process. A discussion about this family rule offers family members insight regarding the denial process that is a natural consequence of living with addiction.

Didactic

The Don't Talk Rule is the king in the addictive family. This doesn't mean people literally don't talk, it means that they learn how not to talk honestly about things they see, hear, feel, and think.

Family members learn the Don't Talk Rule for a variety of reasons that in the past have made sense, but now, at this stage, it only enables the family disease and impedes recovery.

The predominant reasons for ascribing to the Don't Talk Rule were:
1. You tried talking about what was happening but it did no good at the immediate moment, so you quit trying.
2. You tried talking about what was happening and, in fact, things got worse; that is, there was yelling, screaming, threats.
3. You didn't know what to say, didn't understand what was happening. "I can't make sense out of it, it is hard for me to describe." So, you didn't talk.
4. No one else talked about it. When you didn't hear others talking about it, you rationalized there must be something wrong with you, or there wouldn't be any support if you did talk about it.
5. You felt you were betraying the person you care about and love. This is the foremost reason family members quit talking about what is happening.

You betray yourself when you do not speak your truth. You are not betraying the addict by talking honestly; when you speak your truth you are betraying the addiction.

Begin a discussion about denial by normalizing it as a natural consequence to a confusing, fearful, troubled situation. Explain that denial is a defense—an attempt to bring stability into one's life. Because denial is a word that may have a negative connotation, other words such as minimize, discount, or rationalize may help a family member to recognize denial. Rather than ask, "What have you denied?" ask, "What situations or feelings have you minimized, discounted, or rationalized?"

More often than not people realize the addicted person is in denial. Denial is a natural part of any addictive disorder, it is pivotal to the addict being able to rationalize and continue with the behavior. In essence the addict says, "I am not drinking too much and I need to drink this much because . . ." This distortion of perception and logic is central to the addiction.

But denial is not unique to the addicted person. If it were, addicted persons would quickly become isolated, anxious, and upset because their behavior and explanations would be unacceptable to those who count in their lives. But the people close to the addict often come to think the same way; they echo the explanations of the addicted person. They minimize, discount, rationalize, and deny. As one young child said, "In our family we just pretend things are different than how they really are."

The addicted family is dominated by their focus on addiction and its denial that is supported by a strong belief in control. The addict maintains two core beliefs: I am not an addict; I can control my behavior. These beliefs form the heart of the addict's identity and view of self. Incoming data must be altered to fit these core beliefs, or else be ignored, or denied. These beliefs are at the core of the family story as well. The addiction, the chaos, inconsistency, and unpredictability are denied; they become incorporated in the family's sense of normality or are attributed to some other problem.

All human beings employ mental maneuvers called defenses. Defenses are devices that all of us use to tamper with reality, or to avoid pain. They work as painkillers; they create blind spots in our perception and awareness. Any reality that is difficult, undesirable, threatening, or painful can then be put in its place. Defenses help to sidestep, minimize, explain away as something else, or simply deny and reject what is happening. While we all exercise normal human defenses, what makes them problematic for the addicted person and the family is the degree to which they routinely operate and must be relied on.

To deny requires dishonesty. Honesty sabotages any immediate attempts to bring consistency or predictability to a very chaotic and confusing family, and when it is applied in traumatic situations, it often causes discomfort and uproar. On a long-term basis, though, it produces stability and promotes health for the individual and family system.

Introduce the handout *Minimizing – Discounting – Rationalizing*. After family members complete it, discuss it. Encourage them to identify five to ten examples of their minimizing behaviors.

Optional: Ask participants to create a collage that depicts their denial. A collage is made by taking pictures, words, and/or letters from magazines to make a statement. Depending on time, offer participants twenty to thirty minutes to create their collages. Suggest they begin by flipping through a magazine and being open and receptive to what they see rather than looking for specific words or pictures. Instructions don't need to be any more specific. This will allow the participants to be more spontaneous which often results in them sharing more freely. If they have not made a collage before and are hesitant, then share some representative examples.

Examples: A picture of . . .
1) Food may represent using food as a defense to medicate feelings.
2) A person smiling may represent projecting the feeling of happiness when one is actually depressed.
3) A gun may represent a situation charged with fear and violence that was never talked about. (A gun may not have been a part of the situation, but is used symbolically.)

Remind participants that these are their collages. Only they will interpret the pictures and/or words. There is no right or wrong way to complete a collage.

Have each participant describe his/her collage, discussing insights and feelings.

Minimizing – Discounting – Rationalizing

Complete the following sentences about separate occasions.

I have minimized, discounted, or rationalized _____

_____

when in reality _____

_____

I have minimized, discounted, or rationalized _____

_____

when in reality _____

_____

I have minimized, discounted, or rationalized _____

_____

when in reality _____

_____

I have minimized, discounted, or rationalized _____

_____

when in reality _____

_____

Powerlessness and Unmanageability

Family Objectives

To recognize powerlessness in the face of addiction.

To identify unmanageability.

Materials Needed

Handout – Family Powerlessness and Unmanageability

Handout – Preoccupation and Effects

Starting Point

In spite of tremendous efforts to help family members discontinue enabling behaviors and help them recognize the disease is not about their behavior, they continue to enable. They continue to think they are responsible, if not for somehow causing the addict to act out, then for not stopping the addictive behavior. This session offers a slightly different angle in helping family members grasp the basic Al-Anon principles of powerlessness and unmanageability. By accepting and identifying with these principles, they are more apt to quit enabling and can step outside the shadow of addiction to reclaim their own lives.

Didactic

The ultimate consequence of codependency is that life becomes controlled by someone else's addiction. One of the most important messages you need to grasp is that you are powerless over anyone's addiction. Without a firm grasp of this concept, you will stay controlled by the disease and you will continue to enable.

The bottom line of recovery for the addicted person is the need to accept that he or she is genuinely powerless over the addiction. Recovery for your family begins with your acceptance that you are powerless over the addicted person's usage or behavior. That means you need to come to terms with the fact that no amount of controlling, begging, pleading, or manipulating will keep the addicted person clean and sober, to truly know in your heart and soul the addicted behavior is not about you; it is about the addict and his or her disease. For some family members, realizing they are powerless can feel like a slap in the face, while others may feel powerless and have been overcome with helplessness for a long time. Do not get confused in the language. Powerlessness is not defeat. The need to recognize that you are powerless does not suggest you jeopardize the financial, physical, and spiritual safety of your family. While you are powerless over the disease that doesn't mean you allow grocery money to be taken and used for drugs; or tell lies for the addict, or sell the car to bail them out of jail, or sign for a home equity loan to pay off their debts.

In the past you may have gone to great lengths to control the addicted person's behavior and usage. That has ended in failure. It may be easier to understand powerlessness if you recognize some of the controlling behaviors you use.

Referring to the *Family Powerlessness and Unmanageability* handout, ask if participants are attempting to take control by using any of the following behaviors. As you name the behavior, direct those family members who identify with it to check it on the handout and share an example of their engaging in this behavior.

- Silent Treatment
- Lying
- Making Threats
- Accommodating
- Canceling Plans
- Assuming Responsibilities

- Pretending
- Lecturing
- Avoiding
- Relocating
- Hiding or Dumping (alcohol, drugs, food, sex paraphernalia, etc.)

Now, have them go back and check boxes in the column headed, *In the long run did it make a difference?* It is important to emphasize *in the long run* because in the short run sometimes it was helpful in a crisis. But in the long run control attempts were not effective. Begin a discussion, asking participants to share what they have identified.

Validate that these behaviors are to be expected when you care about someone who is addicted. Getting control is very often an attempt to bring order to chaos, to bring comfort to pain, but it is important for family members to see that in spite of their best efforts the situation just continues to worsen.

In addition to recognizing and accepting powerlessness, family members need to recognize the unmanageability of their lives. In Al-Anon this is addressed in the first step: "We admitted we were powerless over alcohol—that our lives had become unmanageable." The word *unmanageable* is hard for an individual to grasp when in fact he or she may be the one person in the family who has worked so hard to keep things in order. Yet they pay a price. That is what you want them to recognize, that unmanageability represents the price they pay, the negative consequences to their self—their emotional, mental, physical, and spiritual self.

Return to the handout and review the *Unmanageability* section. Now ask participants to check any of the consequences that apply to them under *Unmanageability*.

- Loss of Sleep—lying awake waiting for them to come home
- Headaches—often stress-induced
- Stomach Problems—stomach is in a constant knot
- Destructive Eating Patterns—eating as a source of comfort, or eating in anger—not eating when nervous or angry, which can frequently result in weight change

- Inappropriate Expression of Anger—directing anger toward the wrong person, being verbally abusive, physically abusive
- Silent Rage—the anger and rage is felt by all but never spoken out loud
- Excessive Crying—finding yourself crying frequently and even not knowing why
- Isolation—finding yourself avoiding family and friends
- Job Impact—performance or attendance impaired
- Martyrdom—going on a shopping spree spending their money, having an affair
- Mental Impairment—inability to focus attention
- Total Preoccupation—with this problem to the exclusion of other aspects of life
- Destructive Behavior—against yourself or another
- Abuse of Alcohol or Drugs
- Depression
- Other

Continue the discussion by incorporating what the participants have identified in this last segment of the handout. Remember that this may be the first constructive discussion they have had about their own unmanageability.

When addiction begins to pervade one's life, one's behavior can change so gradually that it may go unnoticed. Pretty soon it is as if you are a whole different person than you remember once being. You feel, think, and act in ways that don't feel good. This is what is meant by unmanageability.

By identifying where you have the power to effect change, and where you do not, you will come to find your strength. The Serenity Prayer is a popular prayer used by many people in recovery today. *God grant me the serenity to accept the things I cannot change, the courage to change the things I can, and the wisdom to know the difference.* (Reinhold Niebuhr 1892–1971)

Pull the two concepts of powerlessness and unmanageability together by reminding participants—"While you are powerless over the disease, you are not powerless over your behavior."

To facilitate engaging family members in a discussion about powerlessness and unmanageability, an additional format is the handout *Preoccupation and Effects* given as an assignment. If the handout is the focus for a session, give participants fifteen minutes to complete it and then begin a discussion.

Family Powerlessness and Unmanageability

ATTEMPTS TO GET CONTROL	IN THE LONG RUN DID IT MAKE A DIFFERENCE?		UNMANAGEABILITY
☐ Silent Treatment	☐ No	☐ Yes	☐ Loss of Sleep
☐ Lying	☐ No	☐ Yes	☐ Headaches
☐ Making Threats	☐ No	☐ Yes	☐ Stomach Problems
☐ Accommodating	☐ No	☐ Yes	☐ Destructive Eating Patterns
☐ Canceling Plans	☐ No	☐ Yes	☐ Inappropriate Expression of Anger
☐ Assuming Responsibilities	☐ No	☐ Yes	☐ Silent Rage
☐ Pretending	☐ No	☐ Yes	☐ Excessive Crying
☐ Lecturing	☐ No	☐ Yes	☐ Isolation
☐ Avoiding	☐ No	☐ Yes	☐ Job Impact
☐ Relocating	☐ No	☐ Yes	☐ Martyrdom
☐ Hiding or Dumping (alcohol/drugs/ sex paraphernalia/food/etc.)	☐ No	☐ Yes	☐ Mental Impairment
			☐ Total Preoccupation
			☐ Destructive Behavior
			☐ Abuse of Alcohol or Drugs
			☐ Depression
			☐ Other (name)

Preoccupation and Effects

Preoccupation
- When did you become aware that the addict was preoccupied with his or her addictive behavior?

- When did you become preoccupied with the addict and his/her behavior?

Attempts to control
- When did you first begin to try to control the use of alcohol, other drugs, or other addictive behavior?

Insane behavior
- Describe at least three things you would not have done if you had not been preoccupied or obsessed with their behavior.

Personal effects
- When did you begin to: "walk on eggshells"; repress your feelings; increase your own use of alcohol or other drugs or other self-medicators, such as overeating, excessive shopping, revenge affairs; use or engage in behavior similar to the addict?

- In what ways has your behavior had a negative impact on your physical health, feelings about yourself, your work?

Enabling

Family Objectives

To identify enabling behaviors.

To recognize the futility of enabling behaviors.

Materials Needed

Handout – The Enablers

Handout – Enabling Exercise for Addict

Handout – Enabling Exercise for Family

Starting Point

This session offers an understanding of enabling behavior and gives family members an opportunity to identify for themselves what behaviors they engage in that support the addiction and sabotage recovery for themselves and the addict. It is only when family members understand that they are truly powerless and their lives have become unmanageable that they have the willingness to genuinely stop enabling behaviors. Therefore it is necessary to assist them in identifying with their powerlessness and unmanageability prior to beginning a discussion about enabling behavior.

Didactic

Enabling behavior is most often fueled by love and/or fear. It is normal behavior in the face of dealing with the unidentified scary behaviors of addiction, yet it only supports the addiction. To no longer support the addiction and to no longer allow the disease to be central to your life it is vital you practice what is called tough love. Tough love means to let go of enabling behavior—behavior that makes it easier for the addicted person to escape the consequences of their addictive disorder.

Examples of enabling behavior are:
- Covering up for the addicted person
- Lying
- Making excuses
- Loaning money
- Bribing
- Cleaning up
- Maintaining the Don't Talk Rule

Ask family members—individually, with family, or in a group—if they can identify what behaviors they use that protect the addicted person. *The Enablers* handout may assist them in identifying enabling behaviors. This dialogue is most powerful in a group with other family members as they can see themselves as they listen to others having done identical behavior. They don't feel the shame as much when they hear other family members say they have done the same or similar behavior.

The enabling process is any behavior that supports the delusion that the addiction is not the problem and aids the addicted person in avoiding responsibility for his/her addiction-related behavior. You need to practice tough love. Tough love means allowing the addicted person to experience the consequences of his/her behavior. It is called tough love because it is difficult to see the addicted person in pain. You may be confused; you may feel guilty. It is not easy to quit enabling, but when you attempt to shield or protect the addict from his/her own behavior, you are only protecting the addiction.

If you carry a toddler everywhere because you don't want them to risk falling and being in pain, that child will never learn to walk. He or she wouldn't learn the basics of needing to step a little higher to go up the stairs. It is important not to get in the way of what the child needs to learn. As it applies to a child it applies to the addicted person. Getting in the way of negative consequences does not rescue the addicted person; it only rescues the addiction.

The family can love the addicted person, but tough love them—that is love them in their hearts but stop any behaviors that make it easier for them not to feel the consequences of their addiction.

Optional: After a discussion on enabling, utilize the handouts *Enabling Exercise for Addict* and *Enabling Exercise for Family*. (This exercise can only be effective if the addicted person is in treatment and/ or early recovery and is desirous of recovery.) The enabling exercise can be done with individuals, in family session, or before whole groups. Ask each participant to complete the respective handout. If you are working with one addicted person and three family members, the addict will complete a handout specific to each family member present, while each family member only completes one.

If there is any concern that the addict won't be able to identify enabling behaviors, understand that he or she has been relying on these behaviors. Any resistance to identifying such behavior stems from wanting the enabling to continue—"If I don't tell them how they enable me, they just might continue to do it."

The greatest power in this exercise lies in the family hearing the addict recognize how he or she has been enabled. The addict always shares first. (Addict to first family member, then that family member to addict; then addict to second family member, then that family member to addict, until all have taken their turn.) Addicts can identify how they have been enabled, and as they verbalize it to their family, it helps the family to realize how their behaviors simply reinforce the addictive behavior. To stop enabling behavior it is necessary to have more than an intellectual understanding. While family members have been enabling from a position of fear and love, this exercise frequently helps them to realize they are being used and manipulated, which boosts their willingness to stop the hurtful enabling behavior. This tool makes tough love behavior more possible.

The Enablers

Who are the enablers? They are those persons in the addict's life who, by their actions and words, enable him or her to continue the same patterns of chemical use and/or actions. The enablers are the spouses, partners, parents, children, friends, employers, doctors, police, judges, and all other persons who shield the addicted person from the consequences of the addictive behavior. Change in behavior is motivated by discomfort. Shielding the addict from "discomfort" makes it easier for the use and/or actions to continue. The following examples are enabling actions and responses that allow the addicted person to escape the responsibility and discomfort of the addiction behavior:

1. Borrowing money to pay bills because the addicted person neglected to pay them, or used the money to buy chemicals, sex, or to gamble, etc.
2. Calling the addicted person's work and providing an excuse for his/her absence because he or she is sick or has not come home due to addictive behavior.
3. Asking for help from clergy, police, or lawyers to get the addicted person off a legal or criminal charge related to the addiction.
4. Telling friends that you can't attend a party or social function because a child is sick, or the babysitter canceled, etc., rather than tell the truth about the addicted person's behavior.
5. Making excuses to people for the addicted person's inability to carry through on a job or responsibility.
6. Loaning the addicted person money, paying his/her bills, financing major aspects of his or her life while he or she continues to act out and has not engaged in a recovery program.
7. Making excuses for the addicted person's behavior and/or reinforcing the addicted person's excuses, that is, "if only he had been a stronger child," "she was a sensitive youngster," "he married the wrong woman," "his father ignored him," "the teachers never liked her," "other kids always teased him," etc.
8. Denying that the addicted person has an addiction.
9. Drinking, using, and/or engaging with the addicted person around the addictive behavior.
10. Minimizing: "It's not so bad." "Things will get better when . . ." and/or justifying the addiction by agreeing with the rationalizations of the addict.
11. Taking over the addicted person's responsibilities.
12. Avoiding discussing problems with the addicted person.
13. Avoiding contact with the addicted person and making excuses to stay away from home rather than admitting that he or she is making home life uncomfortable.
14. Purchasing a stash for the addicted person.
15. Putting the addicted person to bed, picking up after him or her and not speaking about it at some later time.
16. Lying to parents, friends, or family members about incidents or simply keeping these incidents secret.
17. Not talking about what is occurring.

Briefly stated, the enabling process is any behavior that supports the delusion that the addiction is not the problem and that aids the addicted person in avoiding responsibility for his or her addiction-related behavior.

Enabling Exercise for Addict

Complete this exercise for each family member who is available. While some of the behavior may be the same for different family members it still needs to be listed separately.

Examples of this are . . .

— One of the ways you enabled me was by loaning me money, which I used to buy drugs. What that behavior tells me is that I can get what I want from you.

— One of the ways you enabled me was by not telling anyone how I really broke my leg (falling down the stairs when I was loaded). What that behavior tells me is you'll keep secrets for me so I can keep using.

— One of the ways you enable me is by doing my schoolwork for me when I am behind due to my partying. What that behavior tells me is I can go out and get as high as I want and you'll see that I don't fail my classes.

— One of the ways you enable me is by lying to my boss when I am hungover. What that behavior tells me is I can count on you to cover up my addiction.

Fill in the blanks

1. One of the ways you enabled me was _____

   and that behavior tells me _____

2. One of the ways you enabled me was _____

   and that behavior tells me _____

3. One of the ways you enabled me was _____

   and that behavior tells me _____

4. One of the ways you enabled me was _____

   and that behavior tells me _____

5. One of the ways you enabled me was _____

   and that behavior tells me _____

6. One of the ways you enabled me was _____

   and that behavior tells me _____

Enabling Exercise for Family

Complete this exercise for the addicted person in your family. Examples are . . .

— One of the ways I enabled you was by not telling Mom when you'd sneak out of the house and that behavior tells you and me that it is okay to lie.

— One of the ways I enabled you was by making your house payments for the past two years and that behavior tells you and me that I don't expect you to be financially responsible for yourself.

— One of the ways I enable you is by not telling you when I find your stash and that behavior tells you and me that I am not willing to confront you about your addiction.

— One of the ways I enable you is by not telling your doctor how much you use and that behavior tells you and me that it's okay to continue your substance abuse.

Fill in the blanks.

1. One of the ways I enabled you was _____

    and that behavior tells you and me _____

2. One of the ways I enabled you was _____

    and that behavior tells you and me _____

3. One of the ways I enabled you was _____

    and that behavior tells you and me _____

4. One of the ways I enabled you was _____

    and that behavior tells you and me _____

5. One of the ways I enabled you was _____

    and that behavior tells you and me _____

6. One of the ways I enabled you was _____

    and that behavior tells you and me _____

Now, fill in the sentence *I commit to*. Examples are . . .

— I commit to being truthful.

— I commit to following through with what I say.

— I commit to confronting you rather than remaining silent.

I commit to _____

I commit to _____

I commit to _____

Giving Up Control

Family Objectives

To recognize the meaning of "control" in one's life.

To experience the internal process of letting go of control.

Materials Needed

Handout – Continuum of Control

Handout – Giving Up Control

Starting Point

Often addicts and family members affected by addiction have used controlling behaviors for many years. The need to be in control is a learned response to shame and an attempt to bring order and safety into one's life. To think of letting go of control is very frightening. Yet letting go of control is pivotal to recovery, and very difficult for addicts and family members to grasp. It is not enough to simply tell them it is helpful if they would be willing to let go of control. A discussion on what control means is vital to the process.

Didactic

People learn to control in two ways, often starting in childhood. They control 1) externally, and 2) internally. External control is the manipulation of people, places, and things. Control is a natural learned response to a fearful or chaotic environment. As Chris said, "I raised myself rather well." Tim set the bedtime for his younger brother and sister and made sure they had a bath and were tucked in. He made their lunches for school the next morning. Kimberly would call her father to tell him what he needed to do when he came home from work.

Internal control is the diminishing and/or withholding of feelings and needs, neither expecting nor asking for anything; saying or thinking—

"I am not angry. What is there to be angry about?"

"I wasn't embarrassed. I'm used to those things by now."

"I don't need to go to my friend's house. Who would be home to take care of my sister?"

"I don't want a birthday. Dad wouldn't show up anyway."

This is self-control, protection to ward off further pain by repressing desires and feelings. When you were a child attempts to control internally or externally were about survivorship. It made sense in the context of your environment.

Unfortunately, the continued need for control causes problems in adulthood. Having spent years being hypervigilant, manipulating others and oneself as a way of protection, the controller literally doesn't know how to live life differently. Unfortunately, controllers become so encapsulated and narrow in their view of the world, they don't see what others can so readily see—that they have become authoritarian, demanding, inflexible, and perfectionistic.

Controlling people have difficulty listening, cutting people off in conversations and relationships. They seldom ask for help—can't see options that may be available—have little spontaneity or reactivity—perhaps experience psychosomatic health problems and intimidate people by withholding feelings. Blindly focused on the pursuit of safety and very often unaware of their emotional selves, they are frightened and full of shame relying on what they know best—control. But the consequences are the opposite of what was hoped for as needs do not get met and relationships remain out of balance. Ultimately, hypervigilance becomes burdensome and exhausting. In confusion about what has gone wrong when so much effort was made to make things right, the controlling person can easily succumb to depression and may resort to unhealthy ways of coping with sadness and pain that often result in addictive behaviors.

The handout *Continuum of Control* helps family members to understand how control issues are manifested in rigid and chaotic families in contrast to healthier functioning families.

Letting go of control is often extremely difficult to do. Addicts and codependents re accustomed to trying to control every aspect of their lives—people, places, and situations. In order to embrace recovery, it is necessary to surrender to the fact that one is powerless over people, places, and situations. In surrendering, a great deal of fear may surface at the thought of what might happen if control were given up.

The handout *Giving Up Control* is designed to help identify unspoken (and very likely unrecognized) fears of letting go of control. Ask participants to complete the handout and then discuss it, allowing them the opportunity to recognize their barriers and to put any fears into realistic perspective.

Present the concept that letting go of control is also about accepting where their power lies. It is living the Serenity Prayer.

God grant me the

SERENITY to accept the things I cannot change,

COURAGE to change the things I can,

and the

WISDOM to know the difference.

The following imagery helps participants release control and the fear of not having control.

Imagery Direction

When asking people to participate in an imagery, begin by acknowledging that it may feel awkward in the beginning but that it can be highly valuable if they allow themselves to relax and be open to the process.

It is suggested you have soft music playing in the background. The key is for the presenter to talk slowly, and allow the participants time to breathe deeply, to hear the words, to be with the words. It is not necessary to have a discussion about the imagery once completed. In fact, that is often contraindicated because it moves the participant from an emotional/spiritual experience into an intellectual realm.

Begin the experience by asking the participants to find a comfortable sitting position, uncross their arms and legs, and begin to take slow deep breaths in and out. As you offer these directions, begin to pace your speaking so that it is soothing and relaxing.

Letting Go of Control Imagery

Sit down in a quiet, comfortable place. Uncross your arms and legs and gently close your eyes. Breathe in and out deeply and slowly. As you breathe in, visualize healing energy coming into your body. As you breathe out, imagine stress and tension slowly leaving your physical self.

Become aware of your feet on the floor. Gently move them around and feel the connection between your body and the earth. Visualize your connection with the earth and allow yourself to slowly breathe in and out. As you breathe, continue to let any stress and tension melt away.

Now slowly become aware of your legs. Breathe healing energy into your legs and feel the safety and warmth of that healing energy. Slowly feel the energy as it moves up from your legs . . . to your waist . . . into your chest and around into your back. Feel the muscles in your back relax as your body floats freely.

Be aware of your breathing as you breathe in . . . and out. Feel your arms and shoulders. Feel your shoulders loosen as the stress leaves them . . . feel the healing energy penetrate to your deepest muscles. Feel your neck begin to relax as you continue to breathe in healing energy. Feel your head relax, as the stress continues to be released throughout your body.

Take a deep breath in . . . now out.
Take a deep breath in . . . now out.
Take a deep breath in . . . now out.

As you sit in your calm and safe place, repeat the phrase
    Today, I will release my need to be in control.
    Today, I will release my need to be in control.

Continue to be aware of your breathing. Breathe in . . . and out. Breathe in . . . and out.

As you repeat this phrase, breathe in protection and strength. As you breathe out, release any fears you have about losing control.

Say to yourself

> *I am powerless over people, places, and situations.*
> *I am powerless over people, places, and situations.*

As you continue with your breathing, scan your body again for any feelings that may be surfacing. Allow those feelings to come up in your body. Know that it is okay to feel whatever you are feeling and that you are completely safe. Breathe into those feeling places and breathe out the energies of long held feelings. Breathe in light, healing, and protection. Know that you are safe and that any feelings that may be coming up are safe to have.

Say to yourself

> *I have needed control to be safe.*
> *I have needed control to be safe.*
> *Today I release my fears and I release my control.*
> *Today I release my fears and I release my control.*

Visualize control and fear leaving your body, floating up and away. Feel the weight of needing to control leave your body. Continue to breathe in . . . and out. Breathe in . . . and out.

Say to yourself

> *I am in a safe place and no one can hurt me.*
> *I am in a safe place and no one can hurt me.*

Know that your Higher Power is protecting you and guiding you on your recovery journey. Visualize the energy of your Higher Power protecting you, keeping you safe, and guiding your path.

Say to yourself

> *Today, acceptance is the answer to all my problems.*
> *Today, acceptance is the answer to all my problems.*
> *Nothing happens in this world by mistake.*

As you say these words, allow your spirit to hear the words and accept that none of us have any control over people, places, or situations.

Say to yourself

> *I am powerless over people, places, and situations.*
> *Today, acceptance is the answer to all my problems.*
> *I am powerless over people, places, and situations.*
> *Today, acceptance is the answer to all my problems.*

As you continue to breathe deeply, become aware of your body. Become aware of your head . . . your neck . . . your shoulders and arms. Become aware of your back . . . your chest . . . your waist . . . your legs . . . your feet. Gently begin to shift your body around and when you are ready, open your eyes.

Continuum of Control

Control Issues in Rigid, Chaotic, and Healthy Families

1 — — — — — — — — 2 3 4 5 6 7 8 9 — — — — — — —10

No Control "1"	Some (S-O-M-E) Control "2 – 9"	Total Control "10"
Family of origin: Chaotic; extreme disorder. Rigid controls attempted to create some safety Abandonment experiences All or nothing thinking Survival dependent on following family rules superimposed on chaos to create appearance of order Family rules: Don't talk; Don't trust; Don't feel Belief: Life is unmanageable	"Normal." Some order; some disorder. Control not a central family issue Few, if any abandonment experiences Life is not experienced as "all or nothing" but a process Survival or parental approval not dependent on family rules Family behaviors: Talk; Trust; Feel Belief: Some things in life can be managed; some cannot	Rigidity; no apparent disorder. Hidden feelings grow chaotic & threaten to emerge, trigger chaotic events Abandonment experiences All or nothing thinking Parental approval and protection dependent on following family rules prohibiting natural disorder Family rules: Don't talk; Don't trust; Don't feel Belief: Life is a matter to be managed
In Adult Life: Fear of loss of control of self, fear of feelings Fear of being abandoned by loved ones Attempts to control based on past beliefs, feelings, and behaviors or to act out chaos External approval sought for beliefs and behaviors Poor Inner Adult recovery skills	Loss of control is not primary fear. Confident and accepting of self and feelings Not driven by fear of abandonment. Trust self and others Recognition of where you have the power to affect things and where you don't Internal reference for feelings, behaviors, and beliefs Activated Inner Adult skills: validate self, let go of control, feel feelings, identify needs, set limits and boundaries	Fear of loss of control of self, fear of feelings Fear of being abandoned by loved ones Attempts to control based on past beliefs, feelings, and behaviors or reject all control External approval sought for beliefs and behaviors Poor Inner Adult recovery skills

Giving Up Control

Complete this sentence stem.

Giving up control in my life would mean . . .

1. _____

2. _____

3. _____

When I think about giving up control, my fear is . . .

1. _____

2. _____

3. _____

Powerlessness and Control

Family Objective

To further recognize powerlessness over addictive disorders.

Materials Needed

Handout – Control

Collage materials for each participant: 3 to 5 magazines (nearly any magazine can be used; it is suggested that there be an assortment)

14" x 17" pieces of paper, scotch tape, scissors

Starting Point

An additional tool to facilitate family members' recognition of their powerlessness and be more motivated to change their behavior is the *Control* handout. The questions posed in the handout could be included in other related sessions or simply used to facilitate discussions at other strategic times. The first question begins the dialogue. It's a pat question in that the obvious answer involves "the addicted person." The second question allows them to be more specific about how they demonstrate controlling behavior. Without being able to identify specific behaviors, one won't be able to focus on those areas that need change. The third question is the motivator. If they do not recognize the consequences of their behavior, they won't be motivated to change.

A collage is another powerful way for family members to express themselves. Ask participants to create a collage of their powerlessness and inability to control. A collage is made by taking pictures, words, and/or letters from magazines to make a statement. Depending on time, offer participants twenty to thirty minutes to create their collages. Suggest they begin by flipping through a magazine and being open and receptive to what they see rather than looking for specific words or pictures.

Examples: A picture of . . .
1. A person with food smeared all across his/her face may represent powerlessness around addiction.
2. Cars, clothes, and boats may represent compulsive buying sprees in response to feeling powerless.
3. An empty bottle may represent powerlessness over the alcoholic.

Remind participants this is their collage. Only they will interpret the pictures and/or words. There is no right or wrong way to complete a collage. Have each participant describe their collage, discuss insights and feelings.

Control

1. What aspects, situations, or people in your life are you experiencing difficulties with because you are trying to control that which in fact you do not have the power to control?

   _____

   _____

   _____

   _____

   _____

2. How are you demonstrating this controlling behavior?

   _____

   _____

   _____

   _____

3. What is the price you pay for this behavior?

   _____

   _____

   _____

   _____

Codependency First Step

Family Objective

To recognize and come to a greater acceptance of being powerless over anyone else's behavior or addiction.

Materials Needed

Handout – Codependent Checklist

Handout – Codependent Questionnaire

Starting Point

In the early stages of treatment, the addicted person is often asked to identify behaviors that represent his or her powerlessness over the addiction and how life has become unmanageable. In Twelve Step programs this is known as the First Step. This session, for family members only, is similar in that they need to identify and explore in depth the codependent behaviors that represent their powerlessness around the addiction and how their lives have become unmanageable. Doing so helps to reinforce their need for a recovery process. The *Codependent Checklist* handout can be done quickly and is a warm-up exercise for the more thorough *Codependent Questionnaire*, which is best given as an assignment as it could take a few hours to complete. The questionnaire can be used as the outline for participants writing out their Step One. Ask each participant to share his or her completed questionnaire with a counselor or in a peer group, as it is not meant to be shared with the addicted person.

This session is best conducted after covering the material in the previous sessions in this section.

Codependent Checklist

The following are typical co-addictive traits. Simply check off those traits that apply to you. The more items you check, the more you will see a co-addictive pattern in your life.

☐ Concealing behavior of the addict

☐ Denial of the obvious

☐ Intense mood swings from high to low

☐ Self-righteous criticism and judgment of the addict

☐ Rationalizing addict's behavior

☐ Belief that if addict changed, all problems would disappear

☐ Strategies to control sexual activity of addict

☐ Being sexual with the addict to prevent the addict from being sexual with others

☐ Feelings of depression and remorse

☐ Loss of friendships

☐ Secret pacts with other family members

☐ Distrust of each other within the family

☐ Growing self-doubt and fear

☐ Neglect of spiritual pursuits including prayer or meditation

☐ Changes in eating or sleeping patterns

☐ Loss of time on the job

☐ Ongoing list of resentments and disappointments

☐ Increasing financial problems

☐ Overextension and over involvement in work or outside activities

☐ Feelings of superiority to addict

☐ Alibis, excuses, and justifications to others

☐ Overlooking addict's behavior

☐ Protecting the addict from consequences of behavior

☐ Distrust of others outside the family because of addict

☐ Attempts to "catch" or trap the addict

☐ Efforts to threaten or exact promises from the addict

☐ Feelings of responsibility for addict's behavior

☐ Fantasizing and obsessing about addict's problem

☐ Suicide attempts or thoughts

☐ Deterioration of family "pride"

☐ Feeling distant from other family members

☐ Loss of self-esteem or self-respect

☐ Feeling unique

☐ Accidents, illnesses, or injury due to the stress of addiction

☐ Unusual dreams

☐ Decreased ability to work or function

☐ Efforts to control family expenditures with increasing failure to do so

☐ Takeover of duties and responsibilities of addict in effort to keep family life "normal"

☐ Engaging in self-defeating or degrading behavior

Codependent Questionnaire

"We admitted we were powerless over addiction and that our lives had become unmanageable."

Have you really accepted the fact that you cannot control another person's addiction? Are you willing to carry this acceptance a step further by admitting you are powerless over anyone but yourself?

The following questionnaire will help you understand your own codependency issues. On a separate piece of paper give at least three specific examples in each area. There are no right or wrong answers, only your answers.

1. Preoccupation with the addict: When did you become aware that your family member was preoccupied with drinking or using, or engaging in other addictive behaviors? When did you then become preoccupied with the behaviors? When did you begin to "walk on eggshells?" Repress your feelings? Increase your own self-destructive behaviors?

2. Attempts to control: When did you first begin to try to control the addict or addictive behavior by: a) getting rid of supply; b) buying in an attempt to control the supply; c) punishing the addicted person; d) avoiding social situations where a supply or stash would be present? List other ways.

3. Effects on your physical health: Describe any physical symptoms that may have resulted from your codependent behavior/reactions, such as loss of sleep, headaches, stomach problems, backaches, "nerves," gaining weight, smoking excessively, etc.

4. Effects on your sexuality and sex life: How has the addictive behavior in your relationship affected your feelings about yourself as a man or woman? How has it affected your sexual performance?

5. Effects on your emotional or feeling life: What kinds of feelings did you have about yourself? About others?

6. Effects on your social life and friends: When did you start to make excuses for the behavior to other people? Have you tried to control the type of people you associate with? Have people stopped seeing you because of the problem in your relationship? When have you felt isolated, rejected, or lonely?

7. Effects on your family: How do you think your behavior has affected family members and others who are important to you? For example, do you "take it out" on the kids? Have you become super-parent? Do you overreact? Are you avoiding relatives and family events?

8. Effects on your spiritual life: How has your relationship with a Higher Power been affected? If you have had a religious affiliation in the past, how has this changed?

9. Effects on your work: How has your productivity and output on the job changed? How has your performance as a partner, parent, or student suffered?

10. Effects on your finances: When did you begin worrying or assuming responsibility for financial matters?

11. Effects on your character: People like to think of themselves as responsible, tolerant, generous, honest, etc. As the disease progresses, however, most people find they lose the ability to live up to those standards they value. You may have developed an "I don't care" attitude in areas of your life that were once important. Give at least three examples of values you've let slide as a result of being codependent.

12. Effects on your behavior: Describe at least three things you would not have done if you had not been obsessed with the addicted person's behavior.

13. Have you engaged in destructive behavior against yourself or others such as having an affair, physically assaulting someone, self-mutilation, negative self-talk, attempting suicide, etc.?

Recognizing the Family Dance

Overview

This section focuses on assisting family members in recognizing patterns of relating that are ultimately hurtful to the functioning of the family system. It will help family members identify rigid behaviors and beliefs that intrude on healthy relationships, and offer them models of healthier communication and relating that are crucial to recovery.

Roles help family members to recognize established role patterns that support the addictive family system and lock them into rigid behaviors and beliefs. This session is core to family members recognizing how many of their codependent behaviors were learned and what they can address in their recovery process.

Role Patterns assist in recognizing personal patterns and establishing skill sets for appropriate boundary setting. It is vital family members let go of the rigidity of their individual roles and develop the skills to give themselves choices about how they operate in the world.

Boundaries focus on the ability to identify healthy and unhealthy boundaries. This session is specific about the different types of boundaries—emotional, spiritual, sexual, interpersonal, intellectual, and physical. It culminates with guidelines for communicating healthy boundaries.

Guilt is closely connected with a lack of healthy boundary setting. Family members often assume guilt for other people's behavior, which is false guilt. Delineating true guilt from false guilt is healthy internal boundary protection.

Identifying Boundary Extremes is an extension of the session on boundaries. It facilitates developing a skill set to identify and stop intrusive behavior and high tolerance for inappropriate behavior.

Drama Triangle allows family members to see that by relating without healthy boundaries and not being accountable for self, they perpetuate the family chaos. By relating as a victim, rescuer, or offender, family members can then identify how they enter into the chaotic dance triangle, their "dance" steps, and how to step outside of the family drama.

Secrets are common in addictive families. Letting go of secrets needs to be acknowledged. This session helps family members delineate healthy boundaries that allow for discernment regarding with whom and when a confidence is shared.

Impaired Family is a strong exercise for assisting the family to recognize and take ownership for problems that belong to the entire family. It is most effective with the participation of the addicted person. This session is only helpful to family members after many of the previous sessions have aided them in lessening their denial and establishing greater honesty for their overt behaviors.

Roles

Family Objective

To identify the strengths and vulnerabilities of roles within the addictive family system.

Materials Needed

Handout – Family Roles

Starting Point

Though the addictive family system may continue to function, it is important for family members to understand how a family changes in response to addiction. In addition to the following didactic, the facilitator is encouraged to use whatever materials you value that explain the roles within addictive family systems and help the family realize how they have organized around the addiction. The book, *It Will Never Happen to Me* is an invaluable resource.

Didactic

While one of the clearest indicators of a smoothly working family is constancy, the words that best describe living in a chemically dependent family are inconsistency and unpredictability. What a spouse, partner, or child does while living in an addictive environment they do because at that time it makes sense to them. As the problems surrounding the addiction cause more and more inconsistency and unpredictability in the home, the behavior of the nonaddicted family members typically becomes an attempt to restabilize the family system. Family members in this system act and react in a manner that makes life easier and less painful.

In most well functioning families, one finds emotions being expressed clearly, with each person being given the opportunity to share his or her feelings. Emotions are accepted by an attentive group—one that offers understanding and support. Family members can freely ask for attention, and in return give attention to others. In a home beset by addiction, emotions are repressed and become twisted. Emotions are often not shared, and unfortunately when they are expressed, it is done in a judgmental manner with blame being placed on one another.

While constructive alliances are part of a healthy family, adult members of an addicted family system often lack alliance. If alliances are demonstrated, they are destructive and usually consist of one parent and a child (or children) against the other parent.

Families have rules that need to be fair and flexible. These rules also need to be verbalized. Rules such as "no hitting," or "everyone will have a chance to be heard," lead to healthier functioning within a system. In addictive family structures rules are usually fueled by shame, guilt, or fear. Rather than a verbalized rule that says, "There will be no hitting," there is an unspoken, silent rule that says, "You won't tell others how you got that bruise."

Many times there are clearly defined roles within the family. It is typical for adults in the family to divide or share the roles of being breadwinner and administrator—the one who makes the decisions within the home. Children raised in homes where open communication is practiced and consistency of lifestyles is the norm usually have the ability to adopt a variety of roles, dependent upon the situation. These children learn how to be responsible, to organize, develop realistic goals, play, laugh, and enjoy themselves. They learn a sense of flexibility and spontaneity. They are usually taught how to be sensitive to the feelings of others and they are willing to be helpful. These children learn a sense of autonomy and how to belong to a group. Children growing up in addictive homes, however, seldom learn the combinations of roles that mold healthy personalities. Instead, they become locked into roles they assumed based on their perception of what they need to do to "survive" and bring stability to their lives.

Feeling trapped in a highly confusing system, family members do what is needed to be safe. They do what they need to preserve the family system. Typically this means they hide their feelings behind an artificial behavior pattern. The majority of children tend to adopt one, or a combination, of the following four roles: the *responsible child*, the *adjuster*, the *placater*, or the *mascot*. These are roles that allow children to draw either positive attention or no attention to themselves. A small percentage finds ways to draw negative attention by adopting a fifth role, the *acting out child*. Some children may clearly fit into one or more of these roles. For most, though, there is a primary role, and then secondary roles. Some switch roles. What is important is to identify first the strength and then the vulnerabilities of each role.

An only or oldest child is most likely to be a very *responsible* child. This child not only assumes a great deal of responsibility for him- or herself, but does so for other family members as well. This is the nine-year-old going on thirty-five, the twelve-year-old going on forty. From the onset of addiction in the family, this child has been the adult. It is the seven-year-old putting Mom to bed, the nine-year-old getting dinner ready every night, the twelve-year-old driving Dad around because Dad's too drunk to drive himself, or simply the child whose adult-like behavior is compensating for the parent's immaturity. This role is one in which the child seldom misbehaves, but rather takes on many of the household and parenting responsibilities for the other siblings and, very possibly, for the parents.

Next is the child who is usually not the oldest, nor the only child. This is the child who does not develop the need to be responsible for him- or herself or others. The need to assume responsibility is not as great because there is often an older sibling providing the needed structure in the environment. This middle or younger child finds the best role for him to play is that of the *adjuster*. It is easier to simply follow directions, handle whatever has to be handled, and adjust to the circumstances of the day. This coping pattern allows the child to appear more flexible, more spontaneous, and possibly, more selfish than others in the home.

A third common role within this increasingly chaotic home life is that of the *placater*. This is the family comforter otherwise known as the household social worker. It is this child who often tries to make others in the home feel better as if he or she is responsible for whatever pain the family is experiencing. This youngster is extremely sensitive to other people's feelings, and does what he or she can to lessen the intensity of the pain within the home. The placater is a good listener who can take away Mom's sadness, a brother's fear, a sister's embarrassment, and Dad's anger.

A fourth common role is the *mascot* often referred to as the clown in the family or the family pet. This is the child who brings relief to the family with humor, wit, and cute styles of distraction. The mascot child is often reacting unconsciously to the adage, "If I don't laugh I will cry." Mascots usually receive a lot of reinforcement from others to continue in this role because it provides relief from the pain within the family. Humor and wit lead to positive attention that is extremely important if a child is not getting the attention he or she deserves.

All of these characteristics we can easily find value in and we typically don't see them as destructive. In fact, labeling children with words such as "responsible," "caring," and "able to adjust to crisis" allows them as adults, to pat themselves on the back for having been such good "survivors." The survival mechanisms of those who "look good" often lead to unhealthy extremes. Such unusual development of coping behavior results in emotional and psychological deficits. It is the understanding of such deficits that allows one to understand how survivors end up living out a family script. It is this family script that draws them into their own addictive behavior, marrying someone who is or becomes an addict, or having an unusual number of problems in their adult years.

While most children react to the turmoil in their lives in a way that doesn't draw negative attention to themselves or their family members, a small number of them find ways to say loudly that something is very wrong. Metaphorically and literally they walk through their adolescence, and sometimes their adult years, with a fist clenched and raised and a finger protruding saying, "There is something very wrong in my life and you are going to notice me." Instead of behaving in a manner that actually brings greater stability into their lives, or at least one that does not add to the turmoil, the *acting out child*— the fifth common role, often displays problematic delinquent behavior, behavior that more accurately typifies the true state of the family.

Many various adjectives may have more meaning. Common terms like hero, scapegoat, comic, wallflower, scorekeeper, peacemaker, etc. may apply. What is most crucial to ascertain if you identify with any particular role by any name as a part of responding to an addictive family is to ultimately recognize each role's strengths and vulnerabilities.

The handout *Family Roles* lists common strengths to each role, and common vulnerabilities or deficits. While many people identify with aspects of several roles there are usually one or two predominant roles that need to be the focus. After talking about roles, ask participants what roles they most identify with in their growing up years. Discuss the strengths of their role(s) and where that has aided them in life. Emphasize that the strengths they get to keep. Then focus the discussion on the deficits of their role(s) and how the rigidness of the role(s) has created difficulty in their life. The deficits they identify with will offer them a direction in terms of what to work on in their recovery process. By only looking at their roles' strengths they risk staying in denial about how they have been impacted.

Family Roles

In an addictive or depressed family system the disease becomes the organizing principle. The affected person becomes the central figure from which family members organize their behaviors and reactions, usually in what is a slow insidious process. Typically family members do what they can to bring greater consistency, structure, and safety into a family system that is becoming unpredictable, chaotic, or frightening. In this effort they often adopt certain roles or a mixture of roles.

You are welcome to rename that which best describes you.

RESPONSIBLE/FAMILY HERO

STRENGTHS	DEFICITS
Successful	Perfectionism
Organized	Difficulty listening
Leadership skills	Inability to follow
Decisive	Inability to relax
Initiator	Lack of spontaneity
Self-disciplined	Inflexibility
Goal-oriented	Unwillingness to ask for help
Severe need to be in control	High fear of mistakes
	Inability to play

ADJUSTER/LOST CHILD

STRENGTHS	DEFICITS
Independent	Unable to initiate
Flexible	Withdraws
Ability to follow	Fearful of making decisions
Easy going attitude	Lacking direction
Quiet	Ignored, forgotten, neglected
	Follows without questioning
	Difficulty recognizing choices and options

PLACATER/PEOPLE PLEASER

STRENGTHS	DEFICITS
Caring/compassionate	Inability to receive
Empathic	Denies personal needs
Listens well	High tolerance for inappropriate behavior
Sensitive to others	Strong fear of anger or conflict
Gives well	False guilt
Smiles readily	Anxiousness
Highly fearful	Hypervigilance

MASCOT/FAMILY CLOWN

STRENGTHS	DEFICITS
Sense of humor	Seeks attention
Flexible	Distracting
Able to relieve stress and pain	Immature
	Difficulty focusing
	Poor decision-making ability

ACTING-OUT/SCAPEGOAT

STRENGTHS	DEFICITS
Creative	Inappropriately expresses anger
Less denial, greater honesty	Inability to follow direction
Sense of humor	Self-destructive
Close to own feelings	Intrusive
Ability to lead—just in the wrong direction	Irresponsible
	Social problems at young ages, such as truancy, teen pregnancy, school dropout, addiction, underachiever, defiant, rebellious

While the statements below are subjective generalizations, they describe the reality that many people live.

Examples of beliefs associated with particular roles:

Beliefs of the Responsible Child:
> "If I don't do it, no one will."
> "If I don't do this, something bad will happen, or things will get worse."

Beliefs of the Adjuster Child:
> "If I don't get emotionally involved, I won't get hurt."
> "I can't make a difference anyway."
> "It is best not to draw attention to myself."

Beliefs of the Placater Child:
> "If I am nice, people will like me."
> "If I focus on someone else, the focus won't be on me and that is good."
> "If I take care of you, you won't leave me or reject me."

Beliefs of the Mascot Child:

"If I make people laugh, there is no pain."

Beliefs of the Acting-Out Child:

"If I scream loudly enough someone may notice me."

"Take what you want. No one is going to give you anything."

Examples of responses to feelings as affected by roles:

The Responsible Child:

"I must stay in control of my feelings."

The Adjuster Child:

"Why should I feel? It's better if I don't."

The Placater Child:

"I must take care of others' feelings."

The Mascot Child:

"I must take the pain away."

The Acting-Out Child:

"I am angry about it, whatever it is."

Examples of the way roles dictate how shame may manifest itself in your adult years:

The Responsible Child shows shame with control, perfectionism, and compulsivity.
The Adjuster Child shows shame with procrastination, and victimization.
The Placater Child shows shame with victimization, depression, and perfection.
The Mascot Child shows shame with depression and addiction.
The Acting-Out Child shows shame with rage, addictions, and procrastination.

Original work regarding family roles was done by Virginia Satir, and then adapted by Claudia Black and Sharon Wegscheider-Cruse to fit the addictive family model. Over the course of years the labels vary, yet the descriptions *fit*.

Role Patterns

Family Objective

To identify negative consequences associated with rigid role patterns.

Materials Needed

Handout – The Responsible Child

Handout – The Adjusting Child

Handout – The Placating Child

Handout – The Mascot Child

Handout – The Acting-Out Child

Handout – Present-Day Roles

Starting Point

This material is meant to further the previous session on Roles.

Ask participants to complete the handout(s) of the one or two most predominant role or roles they identify with in their growing-up years. When they have completed their *Role(s)* Handout, each person completes the *Present-Day* Handout. It is most important that they recognize how their childhood role(s) impacts them today.

The ask participants to show their handouts. The facilitator needs to validate the losses incurred as a consequence of rigidly adhering to their role(s).

If the family member is an adolescent, they will need to change the past tense verbiage to present tense on the handouts. For example, *I didn't, I couldn't, I wouldn't,* becomes *I don't, I can't, I won't.*

Have participants identify one or two situations during which they would be willing to relinquish their role(s). Suggest that they begin with a scenario in which they feel they could successfully do this. Explore this by asking them to describe the scenario and then say what they would do differently in that situation. Encourage them to practice new ways of being and relating to assure success with more challenging or threatening situations.

The Responsible Child

The responsible child, otherwise known as the "nine-year-old going on thirty-five," is probably extremely organized and goal-oriented. The responsible child is adept at planning and manipulating others to get things done, placing him or her in a leadership position. This child is often independent and self-reliant, capable of accomplishments and achievements. But because these accomplishments are made less out of choice and more out of a necessity to survive (emotionally, if not physically), usually there is a price paid for this "early maturity."

Complete the following sentences putting yourself back in the realm of your childhood.

1. As a result of being the "little adult" in my family,

    I didn't _____

    I couldn't _____

    I wouldn't _____

2. As a result of being the "little adult" in my family,

    I didn't _____

    I couldn't _____

    I wouldn't _____

3. As a result of being the "little adult" in my family,

    I didn't _____

    I couldn't _____

    I wouldn't _____

4. As a result of being the "little adult" in my family,

    I didn't _____

    I couldn't _____

    I wouldn't _____

The Adjusting Child

The adjusting child finds it easier to not question, think about, nor respond in any way to what is occurring in his or her life. Adjusters do not attempt to change, prevent, or alleviate any situations. They simply "adjust" to what they are told by detaching themselves emotionally, physically, and socially as much as is possible. While it is easier to survive the frequent confusion and hurt of a dysfunctional home through adjusting, there are many negative consequences for the adjusters.

Complete the following sentences putting yourself back in the realm of your childhood.

1. As a result of adjusting/detaching in my family,

    I didn't _____

    I couldn't _____

    I wouldn't _____

2. As a result of adjusting/detaching in my family,

    I didn't _____

    I couldn't _____

    I wouldn't _____

3. As a result of adjusting/detaching in my family,

    I didn't _____

    I couldn't _____

    I wouldn't _____

4. As a result of adjusting/detaching in my family,

    I didn't _____

    I couldn't _____

    I wouldn't _____

The Placating Child

The placater, otherwise known as the "household social worker" or "caretaker," is the child who is busy taking care of everyone else's emotional needs. This is the young girl who perceives her sister's embarrassment when Mom shows up at a school open house drunk and she does whatever is necessary to take the embarrassment away. This is a young boy assisting his brother in not feeling the disappointment when Dad doesn't show up at a ball game. This is a warm, sensitive, listening, caring person who shows a tremendous capacity to help others feel better. For the placater, survival is taking away the fears, sadness, and the guilt of others. Survival is giving one's time, energy, and empathy.

Complete the following sentences putting yourself back in the realm of your childhood.

1. As a result of being the "social worker" in my family,

   I didn't _____

   I couldn't _____

   I wouldn't _____

2. As a result of being the "social worker" in my family,

   I didn't _____

   I couldn't _____

   I wouldn't _____

3. As a result of being the "social worker" in my family,

   I didn't _____

   I couldn't _____

   I wouldn't _____

4. As a result of being the "social worker" in my family,

   I didn't _____

   I couldn't _____

   I wouldn't _____

The Mascot Child

The mascot/comic in the family is often thought of as the family pet. This is the child who shows a strong sense of humor and wit. Their role is to distract from the pain. This method of distraction prevents them and other family members from focusing on the pain. Mascots usually receive a lot of reinforcement from others to continue in this role because it provides relief. Humor and wit lead to positive attention—extremely important to a child who is not getting the attention deserved.

Complete the following sentences putting yourself back in the realm of your childhood.

1. As a result of being the "comic" in my family,

    I didn't _____

    I couldn't _____

    I wouldn't _____

2. As a result of being the "comic" in my family,

    I didn't _____

    I couldn't _____

    I wouldn't _____

3. As a result of being the "comic" in my family,

    I didn't _____

    I couldn't _____

    I wouldn't _____

4. As a result of being the "comic" in my family,

    I didn't _____

    I couldn't _____

    I wouldn't _____

The Acting-Out Child

Some kids become very angry at a young age. Confused and scared, they act out their confusion in ways that get them a lot of negative attention. It is common that they get into trouble at home, school, and often on the streets. These are kids who are behaviorally screaming "there's something wrong here!" These are kids who don't find survivorship in the other roles.

Complete the following sentences putting yourself back in the realm of your childhood.

1. As a result of my acting-out behavior,

   I didn't _____

   I couldn't _____

   I wouldn't _____

2. As a result of my acting-out behavior,

   I didn't _____

   I couldn't _____

   I wouldn't _____

3. As a result of my acting-out behavior,

   I didn't _____

   I couldn't _____

   I wouldn't _____

4. As a result of my acting-out behavior,

   I didn't _____

   I couldn't _____

   I wouldn't _____

Present-Day Roles

Today I am still (check the appropriate boxes)

☐ Overly responsible

☐ Adjusting Placating

☐ Being the mascot / the "clown"

☐ Acting out negatively

Complete the following:

The consequences to this are (i.e., I still have not learned:) _____

_____

_____

_____

Remember, in recovery you don't have to give up the valuable things you learned in your role(s). Balance is your goal. As a responsible child, you won't have to give up your ability to lead and take charge, but you can allow others the opportunity so you have a break. As an adjuster who is super flexible, you can trust your own ability to make decisions and not always be the responder. As a placater, you may retain your sensitivity of these feelings but no longer at your expense. As the mascot, you can retain your sense of humor while being centered and focused. Also as an acting-out child, you don't have to give up your anger, but you can find yourself asking for what you want in a calmer, more direct manner.

Identify three behaviors that will help you move out of the rigidity of your role(s).

1. _____

2. _____

3. _____

Boundaries

Family Objectives

To differentiate unhealthy and healthy boundaries.

To learn how to communicate boundaries assertively.

Materials Needed

Handout – Identifying Boundaries

Handout – Asserting Boundaries

Starting Point

Boundaries are essential to having a healthy sense of self and they are crucial for individual recovery. Because family members have normalized unhealthy boundaries, it is helpful to identify those that are hurtful to themselves and others. In order to stop unhealthy boundary violations they need to be able to recognize them.

Didactic

A boundary is a limit or border that defines one as separate from others—a separate human being, not someone else's possession. There are different types of boundaries. *Emotional* boundaries define the self, ideas, feelings, and values, and you set them by choosing how you allow people to treat you. *Spiritual* boundaries allow you to define the spiritual path for yourself. *Sexual* boundaries limit what is safe and appropriate sexual behavior and offer choices about whom you interact with sexually and the expression of that interaction. *Relationship* boundaries define the limits of appropriate interaction with others. *Intellectual* boundaries provide the opportunity to enjoy learning and teaching and allow you to be curious and inspired. *Physical* boundaries set limits around touch and space.

Unhealthy boundaries create confusion about who is responsible for what, adding to distortion about guilt and shame. As a result of living with chronic boundary violation or distortion, one is often unskilled in setting boundaries or is disrespectful and intrusive of others' boundaries. People who were raised with unhealthy boundaries often normalize hurtful behavior and don't recognize boundary distortion.

It is important to identify the different types of boundaries and offer examples of unhealthy boundary violations. Using the handout *Identifying Boundaries*, ask participants to identify unhealthy and healthy boundaries in each category. To facilitate this process, you can use the following as examples.

Emotional:
> Feelings denied
> Being told what you can and cannot feel
> Being raged at
> Being criticized
> Being belittled
> Lack of expectations
> Being terrorized

Spiritual:
> Going against personal values or rights to please others
> Being taught to believe in a hurtful higher power
> No spiritual guidance
> No sense of prayer or gratitude

Sexual:
> Being sexual for partner, not self
> Lacking sexual information during puberty
> Being given misinformation about your body, your development
> Being shamed for being wrong gender
> Being exposed to pornography

Sexualized comments
All forms of sexual abuse

Relationship:

Falling in love with anyone who reaches out
Allowing someone to take as much as they can from you
Letting others define your reality
Believing others can anticipate your needs

Intellectual:

Being denied information
Not allowed to make mistakes
Not encouraged to question
Being called stupid
Encouraged to follow a parent's dream rather than your own

Physical:

Accepting touch you do not want
Not being taught appropriate hygiene
Violence, pushing, hitting, kicking, pinching, excessive tickling
Being deprived of touch

After each participant has completed the handout and shared his/her responses, conclude with the following remarks.

Boundaries are the mechanisms that bring safety into your life by establishing healthy control. They act as limits for what you will and will not do as well as what you will and will not permit others to do to you. By setting boundaries for yourself, you are exercising your inherent power to declare that you are an autonomous individual in your own right, not a possession or extension of anyone else.

Healthy boundaries are flexible enough that you can choose what to let in and what to keep out. You cannot maintain boundaries without the ability to know your feelings. Feelings are signals for comfort, safety, discomfort, and danger. You want to have boundaries that are flexible but with limits; that move appropriately in response to situations. Boundaries should be distinct enough to preserve your individual self, yet open to new ideas. They should be firm to maintain values and priorities yet open to communicate your priorities. A healthy boundary protects without isolating, contains without imprisoning.

Your ability to protect yourself psychologically and physically is directly related to the firmness of your boundaries. Boundaries bring order to your life. As boundaries are strengthened you gain a clearer sense of yourself and your relationships with others. Boundaries empower you to determine how you'll be treated by others.

Establishing healthy boundaries is vital to recovery, to getting needs met, to developing a sense of self. All of this leads to being strong enough to be able to separate yourself from past shameful messages and behaviors—and to internalize shame no longer.

Developing boundaries means knowing your physical and psychological comfort zone—a safety zone— knowing what you like and don't like. It is having a sense of your own self, separate from others, and is a part of defining who you are.

Optional: If time permits, without having to rush through the previous material, the handout *Asserting Boundaries* is a very useful and important guide to supporting family members in setting and communicating healthier boundaries. Review the handout if there is ample time for discussion, otherwise give it as an assignment and discuss it in the next session.

After reviewing the handout, ask participants to make a list of boundaries they would like to establish and then review their lists with them. Are the boundaries 1) specific, 2) reasonable, 3) enforceable, and 4) logical? Assist them in their goals of healthy boundary setting.

A conclusion to this discussion is to ask participants to identify the thoughts listed in the handout that they identify as being most pertinent to them to use to reinforce maintaining and communicating healthy boundaries.

Identifying Boundaries

Within each type of boundary listed below, identify your experiences with unhealthy boundaries and then with healthy boundaries. Name the person with whom you experienced a boundary violation/distortion and describe the unhealthy boundary. Then name the person with whom you experienced a healthy boundary and give an example of maintaining the healthy boundary.

Emotional

Person _____ unhealthy boundary _____

_____

Person _____ unhealthy boundary _____

_____

Person _____ unhealthy boundary _____

_____

Person _____ unhealthy boundary _____

_____

Spiritual

Person _____ unhealthy boundary _____

_____

Person _____ unhealthy boundary _____

_____

Person _____ unhealthy boundary _____

_____

Person _____ unhealthy boundary _____

_____

Sexual

Person _____ unhealthy boundary _____

_____

Person _____ unhealthy boundary _____

_____

Person _____ unhealthy boundary _____

_____

Person _____ unhealthy boundary _____

_____

Relationship

Person _____ unhealthy boundary _____

_____

Person _____ unhealthy boundary _____

_____

Person _____ unhealthy boundary _____

_____

Person _____ unhealthy boundary _____

_____

Intellectual

Person _____ unhealthy boundary _____

_____

Person _____ unhealthy boundary _____

_____

Person _____ unhealthy boundary _____

_____

Person _____ unhealthy boundary _____

_____

Physical

Person _____ unhealthy boundary _____

_____

Person _____ unhealthy boundary _____

_____

Person _____ unhealthy boundary _____

_____

Person _____ unhealthy boundary _____

_____

Give examples of three boundaries you would like to set.

1. _____

2. _____

3. _____

What is preventing you from establishing these boundaries?

_____

_____

_____

_____

_____

_____

_____

_____

Asserting Boundaries

When setting boundaries—

1. Be specific
2. Be reasonable
3. Make the boundary enforceable
4. Make the boundary logical

Reinforcing thoughts to maintain boundaries—

✓ Remember boundaries are acts of self-care, not attempts to change another person

✓ Stop explaining and justifying

✓ Face your fear

✓ Be honest

✓ Know that "No" is a complete sentence

✓ If you feel guilt when first setting boundaries, feel it and do it anyway

When you . . . (describe the other person's behavior giving specific information)

I feel . . . (use feeling words i.e. angry, sad, pain, anxious, afraid)

I prefer, I want, I need . . . (describe the behavior you are asking for)

When you are prepared to set a boundary—

If you continue . . . (describe the behavior)

I will . . . (describe the specific action you will take to take care of yourself)

Guilt

Family Objective

To distinguish the difference between true and false guilt.

Materials Needed

Handout – Saying No to False Guilt

Handout – Distinguishing True and False Guilt

Starting Point

A significant part of establishing healthy boundaries is recognizing who is responsible for what, and a part of that means being able to distinguish true guilt from false guilt. Family members often assume guilt for other people's behavior. This is false guilt. This session is to give them an opportunity

to recognize the difference in the two types of guilt, owning true guilt while letting go of false guilt.

Didactic

Guilt is the uncomfortable or painful feeling that results from violating your personal standard, hurting another person, or committing an offense. Guilt is a feeling of regret or responsibility about things you have done or didn't do. "I feel guilty when I tell you I will do something and then I don't do it." "I feel guilty for taking something of yours without asking." One is only guilty for one's own behavior or lack of action and is not responsible for other people's addiction or their behaviors. Family members often have a distorted perception of where their power lies and as a result, they live with much false guilt. Distinguishing true and false guilt and saying no to false guilt will help you take ownership for what is yours to own. No longer holding on to false guilt is setting an internal boundary.

Many children have a distorted and almost delusional perception of what they are and are not responsible for. Many struggle with false guilt, to the extreme of believing they are responsible for their parents' drinking or abusive behavior. Jim said, "If I had hidden the car keys, my dad would not have gotten into the car that night. All other times when Dad would go into his drunken rages I would hide the keys. This night I didn't. I was angry. I went to my room hoping he would take the car and kill himself. And he did just that." Jim does not understand that he was not responsible for his dad's death. His dad had a car accident because he was drunk and driving. Jim was thirteen years old and he was frightened and he was angry that night. He could not change his dad's behavior nor was he responsible for it. Today Jim is forty-three years old and he has carried the burden of this false guilt for over thirty years.

Adult children often feel guilty because they drank or engaged in the addictive behavior with their parent. "How can I talk about my mom's alcoholism when I was her drinking buddy? I used to pour her drinks for her." You aren't responsible for your parents' behavior, compulsions, or addictions. Drinking or using with a parent is not a healthy behavior. But it was a way for you to get approval and attention, to have a relationship with your parent. It was a child screaming to get his or her needs met.

The key to separating true guilt from false guilt is recognizing where responsibility lies. False guilt is when you take responsibility for other people's behaviors, feelings, and actions. True guilt is feeling regret for lying, shoplifting, or calling someone a hurtful name. When you are feeling true guilt, you can take actions to take responsibility for your behavior. You may not be able to change how another person feels, but you can express your regret for your behavior, even years after the fact. You can also change your behavior.

Owning and taking responsibility for that which you are guilty not only shows accountability, it is a commitment you are making to yourself that will support your recovery.

The handouts *Saying No to False Guilt* and *Distinguishing True and False Guilt* offer participants the opportunity to develop emotional boundaries, and to let go of ownership of what is not their responsibility. Knowing your participants, make a determination which handout is more relevant. It is not necessary for them to do both of them.

Saying No to False Guilt

It is important to gain a realistic perspective of situations that you have the power to affect. You may have a distorted perception of where your power lies and as a result live with much false guilt. True guilt is remorse or regret you feel for something you have done or not done. False guilt is experienced when you believe you are responsible for someone else's behavior and actions. Because this is usually a lifelong habit it is important to go back and delineate historically what you were and were not responsible for. This assists you in being more skilled at recognizing your lifelong pattern of taking on false guilt and more importantly, stopping it.

Reflect back on your childhood and adolescence and consider the things you feel guilty about and say no to each situation.

Write "No" in the first blank beginning each statement and then continue by finishing the sentence.

1. _____, I was not responsible for _____

   when he or she _____

2. _____, it wasn't my fault when _____

   _____

3. _____, it wasn't my duty or obligation to _____

   _____

4. _____, I was only partially responsible for _____

   _____

Now reflect on your adult experiences and repeat the exercise.

1. _____, I was not responsible for _____

   when he or she _____

2. _____, it wasn't my fault when _____

   _____

3. _____, it wasn't my duty or obligation to _____

   _____

4. _____, I was only partially responsible for _____

_____

You are responsible for your own behaviors and actions. Write down examples of situations for which you are accountable.

1. _____

2. _____

3. _____

4. _____

5. _____

Distinguishing True and False Guilt

Recognizing that you only have the power to affect your own behavior, not the behavior of others, fill in the following sentences.

Today I'm not responsible for _____

_____

when he or she _____

It isn't my fault when _____

_____

It isn't my duty or obligation to _____

_____

I am only partially responsible for _____

_____

I am responsible for _____

_____

I am responsible for _____

_____

Identifying Boundary Extremes

Family Objectives

To identify intrusive behavior.

To identify high tolerance for inappropriate behavior.

To monitor and change boundary violation behavior.

Materials Needed

Handout – Intrusive Behavior

Handout – Tolerating Inappropriate Behavior

Handout – Monitoring Behaviors

Starting Point

This session allows the participant to focus more specifically on unhealthy boundary behavior ranging from being overly tolerant to being highly intrusive of others.

Didactic

Being impacted by addiction in the family, it is common for the addicted person and family members to behave at opposite ends of a continuum, i.e. one is chronically angry while another is anger avoidant. When it pertains to boundaries it is common for one person to tolerate inappropriate behavior while another's behavior is inappropriate and intrusive. It is also possible to swing from one end of the behavioral continuum to another, that is, one moment tolerating inappropriate behavior, the next moment being intrusive and inappropriate. The intrusive person hasn't learned a healthy respect for other people's boundaries and has not learned containment. It is often difficult for the intrusive person to self identify.

113

To intrude is to violate another person's boundaries. Examples of intrusive behavior are 1) meddling or interfering such as offering an opinion about something without being invited, or involving oneself in a situation that does not concern one; 2) overstepping boundaries such as going to a friend's house uninvited and cleaning it because they have an unkempt lifestyle; and 3) caretaking such as attempting to help with what is perceived to be another person's painful feelings before they have even had a chance to articulate what they are feeling. Under the guise of caring and helping, the caretaker is infringing upon what is someone else's feeling to own or share. Intrusive behavior is often rationalized from a stance of caring or helping, and it can be recognized by stopping to check the motivation behind the behavior. Is it a way to be noticed or to receive approval?

With addiction in the family, tolerating inappropriate behavior is a gradual codependent behavior. Tolerance for inappropriate behavior is developed when people have been subject to situations such as lying, drunkenness, verbal abuse, privacy not being respected, etc. The most common response to this is to take on a victim stance in life. High tolerance leads to denial and the inability to recognize inappropriate and hurtful behavior. The troubled family rules, "Don't Talk," "Don't Trust," "Don't Feel," "Don't Think," and "Don't Question," fuel this ongoing tolerance.

Allow participants to choose the handout they most identify with—*Intrusive Behavior* or *Tolerating Inappropriate Behavior*. The handout *Intrusive Behavior* offers the opportunity to recognize and own the boundary violations that are intrusive. *Tolerating Inappropriate Behavior* offers the opportunity to recognize and own a lack of healthy boundary setting.

If working with a family group, ask participants to identify examples of inappropriate behavior and note them on a board. Viewing collective examples is very empowering and enlightening to family members as an alternative to a written assignment.

Journaling is very helpful in that it allows family members to monitor their behaviors daily; recognize feelings or beliefs that fuel a lack of healthy boundaries; and identify healthier boundary behavior. Building on the previous sessions related to boundaries, the *Monitoring Behaviors* handout offers family members a guide to keeping a diary of inappropriate or intrusive behavior and identifying options that would be appropriate responses.

Intrusive Behavior

To be able to recognize intrusive behavior, it is easier to first identify it in others. And if you are intrusive, it is likely that behavior has been modeled for you.

Examples:
- When you wanted privacy while bathing, your mother insisted on being able to enter the bathroom at any time.
- A sister took your toys to her room without asking and didn't return them.
- Dad would walk in and change the television station even though you were engrossed in a show.

List examples of intrusive behavior that took place in your family of origin:

1. _____

_____

2. _____

_____

3. _____

_____

4. _____

_____

As you are identifying intrusive behavior you are learning to identify the "intruding" person.

Name three people with whom you, as an adult, find yourself repeatedly having to say no to or with whom you must set limits:

1. _____

2. _____

3. _____

One could rationalize that these three people have an amazing capacity to ask for what they need; it could be that they are highly intrusive. People can ask for what they need without being intrusive. No one likes hearing a "no" but a healthy person will respect your needs. Intrusive people push for their needs; they do not recognize or care about the needs or rights of others.

You may have practiced intrusive behavior in your adulthood. If you are intrusive, you may not be aware of this behavior. You may have attitudes that incorporate communal ownership. "This is my house, and I can do what I want, when I want." "Being family, they won't mind." "They have a lot of time, so it will be okay." Intrusive people make generalized assumptions that help to assure they get what they want.

If you identify with those attitudes and are questioning whether or not you are intrusive, you may need to seek the help of a close friend. Ask the friend to help you identify those instances when you were intrusive and made assumptions about their time or their belongings.

List four examples of your intrusive experiences:

1. _____

_____

2. _____

_____

3. _____

_____

4. _____

_____

If you identify with a high tolerance for inappropriate behavior, have difficulty knowing what appropriate behavior is, or find yourself being intrusive to others, then the key to stopping this behavior is learning to question. When you are in an uncomfortable situation—STOP.

Ask the following questions,
    "Is this behavior okay with me?"
    "Are they being respectful of my feelings?"
    "Am I being respectful of their feelings and time?"

Tolerating Inappropriate Behavior

Think of situations you experienced as a child and/or adolescent, during which someone else's behavior was inappropriate or hurtful and no one said anything. This is another way of asking yourself, "Was it crazy or hurtful behavior but everyone acted as if it wasn't happening?" List four examples.

1. _____

_____

2. _____

_____

3. _____

_____

4. _____

_____

If you developed a high tolerance for inappropriate behavior as a child it is likely that you continue that pattern today. List examples of situations you have experienced as an adult in which someone's behavior was inappropriate/hurtful but you didn't say anything:

1. _____

_____

2. _____

_____

3. _____

_____

4. _____

_____

Monitoring Behaviors

You may want to keep a daily journal identifying what you have tolerated that was inappropriate or if you need to work on the other side of that continuum, when you have behaved in a manner that might have been intrusive to others. After completing each daily entry, note the feeling experienced in relation to the situation. If there was no feeling, note the fear you would have felt if you had not been so tolerant (or intrusive). Then identify an alternative response.

Examples:

Tolerated Inappropriate Behavior	Demonstrated Intrusive Behavior
I did not stick up for myself when my lover called me a name. *Feeling or attitude:* Hurt, humiliation, anger. *Alternative Behavior:* I could have said, "I am not a dumb . . . (so-and-so)" . . . (then assert my position). OR I could have said, "It is difficult for me to understand your position when you call me names."	I assumed that my sister would babysit for me. I didn't ask ahead of time, although I knew I needed a sitter three days ago. *Feeling or attitude:* Presumption. "She owes it to me because she's my sister." *Alternative Behavior:* Asking my sister if she was available at the time I became aware of my need. OR Never assume my sister is obligated to babysit for me, and always consider it a favor. When I ask her to babysit, I must understand that she has priorities of her own.

SAMPLE JOURNAL ENTRY:

Monday

Tolerated Inappropriate Behavior	Demonstrated Intrusive Behavior
Feeling or attitude: *Alternative Behavior:*	*Feeling or attitude:* *Alternative Behavior:*

Drama Triangle

Family Objective

To identify one's role in unhealthy relational behaviors.

Materials Needed

Handout – Drama Triangle

Large pieces of paper, pens or pencils

Starting Point

People in addictive families often create a triangle of communication that keeps them in a reactive versus authentic style of relating. The Drama Triangle handout is a wonderful tool to help family members recognize unhealthy patterns of communicating and relating. This exercise can be used with an individual only but it is more powerful when done with multiple family members, such as spouses/partners, or parent(s) and child(ren) so that each participant completes a triangle and then shares.

Explain that on each end of the triangle are unhealthy roles that people often engage in—offender, victim, and rescuer. They all serve as training grounds for unmanageability. They prevent psychological equality in relationships and support chaos in family systems.

Victim	Rescuer	Offender
• Receives pity • Is taken care of by rescuers • Controls others by guilt • Avoids responsibility by blaming • Feels helpless and trapped • Presents with lack of personal power • Has low self-esteem	• Feels saintly • Concentrates on others • Is able to avoid self • Gains respect of other rescuers • Feels superior • Gets tired and depleted • Feels unappreciated • Is consumed with resentments • Has low self-esteem	• Avoids discomfort and feelings by offending others • Feels sense of pseudo-power and self-esteem through intimidation • Able to be irresponsible, feel superior, avoid fear • Experiences loneliness • Lacks helpful, honest feedback because of others' fear • Has lack of respect from others • Has low self-esteem

Didactic

Offenders operate from an emotionally competitive dysfunctional power position of "I am okay, you are not okay." They are quick to find fault and be critical; can be bullish, lead by threats and orders; are good at pointing fingers, blaming, and shaming.

Rescuers fail to confront their offenders' inappropriate and/or hurtful behavior. They act as caretakers and people pleasers to lessen conflict and to be the super parent, spouse, partner, child, worker, etc.

Victims/martyrs see themselves as sacrificing for the sake of others, believing they are powerless to take care of themselves.

All three share a lack of boundaries, boundary failure, or are intrusive, and all lack the ability to be intimate or share appropriate feelings.

People enter this triangle from any of the three angles, though most have a common door of entry. Once a person can identify where it is they enter, it becomes important to note how he or she moves around the triangle.

For example:

James enters the triangle frequently as a rescuer. He attempts to rescue his mother from being the victim as she responds to her husband's offender/villain behavior. As he attempts to be the caretaker and rescue his mother, she shifts from being the victim to offender as she begins to say harsh things about his step-dad. James then finds himself rescuing his step-dad. So while James remains the rescuer, his mother has moved from victim to offender and his step-dad has moved from offender to victim.

In this particular family, the mother often enters the triangle as the victim/martyr and then shifts to offender. When she sees her son move to rescue his step-dad (who has now become the victim) she continues in her offender role verbally attacking James who then moves from rescuer into the victim/martyr role.

Sometimes people move all around the three points of the triangle, some move between two points. It is important to recognize that if anyone in this triangle changes roles, the other two roles change as well. As the triangle diagram portrays, remorse and guilt is what often sends the offender to the rescuer role. Resentment sends the rescuer to the victim role and the victim to the offender role.

It is a powerful exercise for family members to draw and identify where and when they enter this cycle and how they move around the triangle depending on the circumstances. Give participants a piece of paper and instruct them to draw a triangle naming the three points of entry. Ask them to give three to five specific examples of times they have entered the triangle and tell what happened. Then discuss with them what they can do to step out of the drama.

The keys to getting out of the triangle are 1) recognizing oneself in the triangle, 2) establishing boundaries, and 3) having realistic expectations of others.

Drama Triangle

Victim / Martyr
It's not fair—everything happens to me—poor me—look at what you made me do, won't take a stand, doesn't respond, simulates compliance, pretends importance

Rescuer
Caretaker, enables, fixes, denies, people pleaser, tolerates, joins in, keeps secrets, doesn't confront, doesn't set boundaries, buys gifts, tries to be super parent, spouse, partner, child, worker, etc.

Offender
Emotional, mental, physical, sexual abuse—drinking, eating, affairs, spending, etc.—passive-aggressive behaviors—critical, teases, shaming, sarcasm, cynicism, patronizing, bully, withdrawing, being late, self-righteous

RESENTMENT   RESENTMENT

GUILT/REMORSE

THE WAY IN

- Unrealistic expectations
- Cognitive distortions

THE WAY OUT

- Explore how I move around the triangle
- Learn to nurture myself
- Practice self-care of body, mind, and spirit
- Take responsibility for myself and stop blaming others
- Have realistic expectations of myself and others
- Learn about boundaries / set and maintain them

Pay-Offs

Victim	Rescuer	Offender
<ul><li>Receives pity</li><li>Is taken care of by rescuers</li><li>Controls others by guilt</li><li>Avoids responsibility by blaming</li><li>Feels helpless and trapped</li><li>Presents with lack of personal power</li><li>Low self-esteem</li></ul>	<ul><li>Feels saintly</li><li>Concentrates on others</li><li>Avoids self</li><li>Gains respect of other rescuers</li><li>Feels superior</li><li>Gets tired and depleted</li><li>Feels unappreciated</li><li>Consumed with resentments</li><li>Low self-esteem</li></ul>	<ul><li>Avoids discomfort and feelings by offending others</li><li>Feels sense of pseudo-power and self-esteem through intimidation</li><li>Able to be irresponsible, feel superior, avoid fear</li><li>Experiences loneliness</li><li>Lacks helpful, honest feedback because of others' fear</li><li>Lack of respect from others</li><li>Low self-esteem</li></ul>

As an adult, I have choices. Getting out of the triangle is a way to get into RECOVERY.

Drama Triangle adapted from a model by Stephen B. Karpman

Secrets

Family Objectives

To recognize that secrets are common in addictive families.

To understand how secrets are harmful to family functioning.

To recognize the importance of releasing secrets.

To identify healthy guidelines for revealing secrets.

Starting Point

The family affected by addiction is often a family riddled with secrets. When people carry secrets, their view of the world is distorted. They are always on the defensive with others, trying to be alert to protect their privacy, and trying to distance themselves from hidden information. They rationalize, distort, and repress information in a way that blocks opportunities for emotional growth and intimacy. Letting go of secrets needs to be discussed early with family members. Be sure to stress confidentiality. (Facilitator: refer to the Confidentiality Notes in the Instructions.) Discuss with family members the need for all to feel that they are in a safe environment. This allows them to share their innermost secrets without fear of shame or breach of confidentiality.

Recovery is about being honest; it is about having healthy boundaries. It is important to help family members delineate healthy boundaries that allow for discrimination with whom a confidence is shared.

The facilitator needs to use his or her best judgment to assess whether or not to address the issue of secrets openly with other family members present or to do so during private individual sessions.

Didactic

It is likely that families affected by addiction have many secrets. When people keep secrets they become adept at rationalizing and tolerating inappropriate behavior. Some secrets are overtly maintained—"No one is to know about this"—other secrets occur as a consequence of having learned the Don't Talk Rule. Also, when people experience something that they do not have language for, they literally can't talk about it and so the experience remains a secret. For example, some children don't identify their being abused because they are taught that physical abuse means being punched or slapped. They don't recognize that having their hair pulled or being slammed up against a wall is abuse. They may believe abusive behavior has to happen every day, so when it only occurs once a month, they rationalize it and it remains a secret.

Family members may live with the secrecy of addiction without knowing it for what it was. Robin said, "I thought my dad was mentally ill. His personality changed so much. I knew he drank a lot, but so did lots of other people we knew. I didn't know he was addicted." This misperception can be even more evident in behavioral addictions such as gambling or sex addiction that may take place out of sight of the family.

The secret may be information that is perceived as shameful or dangerous if others found out. Shame-based secrets could be about problems with the law or having been in jail or prison; or sexual behavior such as extramarital affairs, pornography, pregnancies outside of the marriage, abortions; or of having been subject to physical or sexual abuse. The secret could be emotional, such as a hidden fear, "What if I lose my mind like my mother?" or "I'm questioning my sexual orientation."

For example, Phyllis didn't want her new boyfriend to get close to her family because she didn't want him to know certain things about them, such as her mother's addiction to pills or her brother's abuse of cocaine. As a result, she spent an enormous amount of energy trying to stay separated from a significant part of her life.

Marie had never disclosed that she was sexually abused, and therefore she maintained a barrier between herself and her partner that directly contributed to their sexual difficulties.

Mary—"My mother used to come and cry in my bedroom at night after my father had hit her. When I would ask why she wouldn't leave him or report him to the police, my mother would quickly compose herself. She would tell me, 'Your father just has a small problem with his anger. I don't want anything bad to happen to him.'" In Mary's family, she learned overtly that she had to be the keeper of the family secret and the family shame.

John's family is an example of a covert secret. "Sometimes after school my friends would come over to play. By this time of the day my dad had been drinking for several hours. Often, he would be passed out on the couch when my friends and I came home after school. When my friends would ask what was wrong with my dad, I would say he had a migraine headache and had to take medication. No one ever had to tell me that I needed to make excuses for my dad. I instinctively knew that is what I had to do." John also became the keeper of the family secret and the family shame.

There is a great distinction between a confidence and a secret. A child may be asked to keep the details of a surprise birthday party or vacation from others. The child is being asked to keep a confidence. If others found out, there may be disappointment or loss of the surprise element. The child keeps the confidence because he or she wants to, not because he or she has to. The child often instinctively knows that keeping secrets is not even a choice. It is a matter of personal and family survival. The child is being asked to contain the emotional energy and shame embodied in the secret. There could be overwhelming negative consequences if others found out about the secret.

When family members live a long time withholding information, after a while it just no longer occurs to them to share and confide in others. If something has not been talked about in years, you probably won't think to talk about it now. Years of conditioning to remain closed, protective, and secretive make it highly unlikely that you would choose to share information about present day occurrences that create fear, guilt, or shame.

Carrying a secret is a tremendous burden. There is a great deal of shame inherent in having to keep secrets. As the keeper of the secrets, you feel shame regarding the family member you are keeping the secret about and shame about yourself. You may feel that your value as a person is in question by being a member of such a family.

While secrets can be very powerful because of the control they have, it is often not the content of the secret itself that is so powerful, but what one must do to keep the secret. In an addictive family, it is the proverbial "skeleton in the closet" and everyone in the family is held responsible for remaining on guard in case someone outside the family gets too near the closet.

Secrets need to be told if you are to be free of guilt and pain. However, putting an end to secrets does not mean that all secret things are shared with all people. As you choose safe places and safe people to share with, the word secret dissipates and the word confidence replaces it. Certain secrets may be appropriate for revealing immediately, while others may not be appropriate to reveal to certain people at this time, if ever.

Family Strategies

The benefits of releasing secrets are:
- Relieving a burden
- Allowing you to practice rigorous honesty and be true to yourself
- Preventing a possible surprise discovery
- Empowering you to have a more honest relationship with another
- Stimulating family and personal change
- Reducing risk of relapse

It is always interesting that when you ask family members what their family secrets are, they will often come right out and tell you, as if the secret has been waiting to be exposed with just a simple invitation. Putting an end to secrets does not mean that everything is to be shared with everyone. When exposing secrets, healthy boundaries are important. There needs to be an understanding of why the secret is being exposed and discrimination with whom the secret is being shared.

The sharing of secrets is not an all or nothing phenomena (e.g., I've never told anyone, now I need to tell everyone). Some issues are more personal than others and family members will not want to share them with just anybody. Secrets should only be shared with safe people. Ask family members what secrets they are aware of. As you consider encouraging family members to share secrets, ask them to consider the following:

Who would you like to have this information?
Would you feel safe sharing this information with this person?
Why do you want to share this information with this person?
What has prevented you from telling them?
What do you hope will be the result of sharing this information?
How realistic is that expectation?

The facilitator's role is to help them discriminate what is shared, with whom they share, and the timing of what to share.

The following imagery will help to create ease in letting go of secrets and sharing confidences.

Imagery Direction

When asking people to participate in an imagery, begin by acknowledging that it may feel awkward in the beginning, but that it can be highly valuable if they allow themselves to relax and be open to the process.

It is suggested you have soft music playing in the background. The key is for the presenter to talk slowly, and allow the participants time to breathe deeply, to hear the words, to be with the words. It is not necessary to have a discussion about the imagery once completed. In fact, that is often contraindicated because it moves the participant from an emotional/spiritual experience into an intellectual realm.

Begin the experience by asking the participants to find a comfortable sitting position, uncross their arms and legs, and begin to take slow deep breaths in and out. As you offer these directions, begin to pace your speaking so that it is soothing and relaxing.

Letting Go of Secrets Imagery

Sit down in a quiet, comfortable place. Uncross your arms and legs and gently close your eyes. Begin to allow any tension to dissolve from your body. Breathe deeply and slowly—the worries of the day, the stresses of decisions gradually moving out of your body. Feel a white, healing light around the soles of your feet . . . the energy of the light moving up your legs, through your thighs, your mid body . . . the energy opening and relaxing you as it moves slowly into your chest and heart.

Breathe fully as the light extends down your arms into the palms of your hands and fingers. The light moves into your neck . . . around and up the back of your head . . . down across your forehead into your eyes, soothing every tiny spot behind your eyes . . . let your eyes relax . . . we try so hard to see everything. Feel the light massage your chin and face. Let yourself feel calm, warm, and nurtured as your body relaxes.
Take a deep breath in . . . and out. Take a deep breath in . . . and out. As you sit in your calm and safe place, repeat the phrase—

> *I am not my family's secrets. I am not my family's secrets.*
> *Breathe in . . . and out. Breathe in . . . and out.*

Breathe in protection and strength . . . breathe out the pain and shame of your family's secrets. Say to yourself—

> *I release my family's pain and shame.*
> *I release my family's pain and shame.*
> *I will not carry their shame any longer.*
> *I will not carry their shame any longer.*

Continue to breathe in light, healing, and protection. Know that you are protected and that any feelings that may be coming up are safe to experience. As you breathe, move through your body and become aware of places you are having any particular feelings. When you find such places, breathe deeply and fill those places with light.

Say to yourself—
> *I release this energy. I will no longer carry it.*
> *I release this energy. I will no longer carry it.*

Continue to breathe in . . . and out. Breathe in . . . and out.

Say to yourself—
> *I am in a safe place and no one can hurt me here.*
> *I am in a safe place and no one can hurt me here.*

Know that your Higher Power is protecting you and guiding you on your recovery journey. Visualize the energy of your Higher Power protecting you and keeping you safe.

Say to yourself—
> *I am not my secrets.*
> *I am not my secrets.*
> *I release their energy.*
> *I will not carry them any longer.*

Breathe in . . . and out. Breathe in . . . and out.

Scan your body again for any feelings that may be surfacing. Allow those feelings to surface. Know that it is okay to feel whatever you are feeling. Breathe into those feeling places and breathe out the energies of long-held feelings.

Breathe in . . . and out. Breathe in . . . and out.

As you breathe slowly and deeply, become aware of your body. Become aware of your head . . . your neck . . . your shoulders and arms. Become aware of your back . . . your chest . . . your waist . . . your legs . . . your feet. Gently begin to shift your body around and when you are ready, open your eyes.

Impaired Family

Family Objectives

To allow every family member to take ownership for his or her contribution to the impairment of the family.

To allow every family member to identify what he or she can do to contribute to the greater health of the family.

Materials Needed

Handout – Impaired Family Board

Starting Point

To reinforce that the family system is the client, taking the focus off the identified addict as the source of dysfunction, the handout *Impaired Family* is an excellent exercise. Using the handout as an example, on a board draw a circle with spokes that represent the number of family members present in this session. To help the family understand the exercise, you may give each participant a copy of the handout and explain.

Example:

The eighteen-year-old son (the person in treatment) contributes to the family impairment with his addiction to alcohol and other drugs. He lies, steals, and is verbally abusive toward his mother and younger brother.

The nineteen-year-old sister contributes by partying with her eighteen-year old brother, and in her anger, she is sullen, sarcastic, and she isolates.

The father does not listen well, he lectures to his wife and the kids. He was not involved in his children's social lives during their childhood years. He also minimizes the drinking and pot smoking that he was aware of with his older son and older daughter.

The mother stays away from the house deliberately, using work as her excuse. She works longer hours than her job requires. She avoids addressing issues with the kids if there is a conflict; and she makes excuses for the kids, overprotecting them, and blaming her husband for their problems.

The sixteen-year-old sister is also using pot and binge drinking. The fourteen-year-old brother isolates by hiding in his room. He knows he's angry, though he isn't sure about what, and knows his hiding is about his anger and uses internet games to release some of his anger.

Begin by asking the family member who is comfortable being first, to go to the board on which you have drawn a circle with spokes and write down the ways in which he or she contributes to the impairment in the family. Continue until all family members present have gone to the board and written the ways in which they, too, contribute to the family impairment.

There may be other behaviors that contribute to the impairment, but this exercise is designed for individual participants to identify the behaviors they are willing to own, and feel safe owning. This is a self-directed activity. Conclude the discussion with each participant identifying what he or she will commit to in order to begin rebuilding a healthier functioning family.

Impaired Family

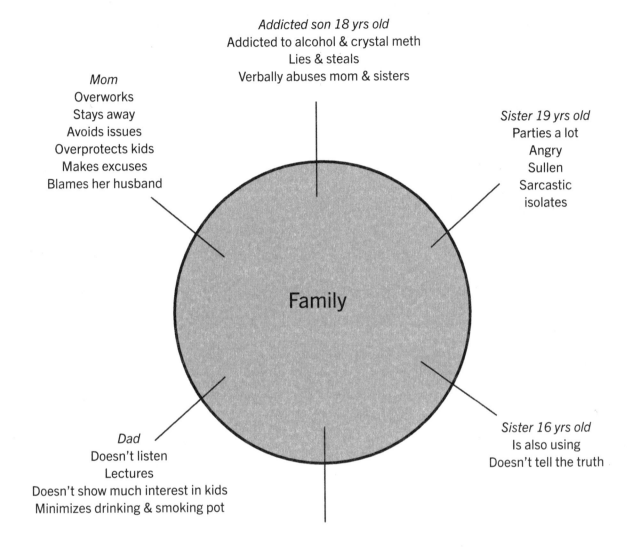

Addicted son 18 yrs old
Addicted to alcohol & crystal meth
Lies & steals
Verbally abuses mom & sisters

Mom
Overworks
Stays away
Avoids issues
Overprotects kids
Makes excuses
Blames her husband

Sister 19 yrs old
Parties a lot
Angry
Sullen
Sarcastic
isolates

Family

Dad
Doesn't listen
Lectures
Doesn't show much interest in kids
Minimizes drinking & smoking pot

Sister 16 yrs old
Is also using
Doesn't tell the truth

Brother 14 yrs old
Silent anger
Hides in his room

Developing Emotional Clarity

Overview

This section offers family members tools to explore and dialogue about their feelings, garner a better understanding of themselves, and develop the capacity to express their feelings in an honest and healthy manner. Beginning with a general exploration of feelings it then becomes more focused on specific feelings, allowing participants to discuss feelings they have toward each other, and aiding them in letting go of more painful feelings. As family members develop greater honesty with themselves and each other, they build greater intimacy as a family unit.

Feelings addresses feelings in general and suggests a variety of dialogues to aid family members in owning their emotions, beliefs about them, and the multigenerational pattern of expression.

Expressing Feelings furthers the discussion of feelings by asking family members to identify emotions that are easily expressed and those that are difficult to express and ascertaining any fears about expressing specific feelings.

Emotional Sociogram is an exercise to help family members recognize the emotional connections between individuals within the family.

Portrait of Feelings suggests creating a collage to allow for a more free expression of family members' relationships with specific feelings. The use of a collage could readily be incorporated into other sessions.

Anger elicits the many unproductive ways anger can be expressed and offers family members the opportunity to identify their thoughts and beliefs about expressing anger. This session also assists in lessening defenses against the healthy expression of anger.

Resentments give family members who are aware of being resentful the opportunity to own their feelings. This session will also assist in developing a structure to be able to let go of resentments and move to a healthier state of relating.

Sadness gives family members the opportunity to identify their thoughts and beliefs about expressing sadness. This session also assists in lessening defenses against the expression of sadness.

Toxic Shame describes unhealthy shame and offers a shame-reduction exercise that helps to lessen a self-perpetuating shame core. This session can easily be combined with *Shame Attacks*.

Shame Attacks needs to follow or be part of the session on Toxic Shame. This session is a practical cognitive-behavioral exercise that family members can incorporate into their recovery skills.

Feelings

Family Objectives

To recognize personal belief systems about expressing emotions.

To identify consequences of those beliefs.

Materials Needed

Handout – Times I Felt

Handout – Feelings Meter

Handout – Willingness to Show Feelings

Handout – Beliefs about Feelings

Board

Starting Point

This is an opportunity to begin the process of talking about feelings. Cultural and familial influences, plus the additional dynamic of reacting to addiction in the family, reinforce negative beliefs about feelings and result in the repression of and/or inappropriate expression of feelings.

Didactic

Being able to identify, tolerate, and express feelings is difficult for many people. Important points in any discussion about feelings are:

- Painful feelings are more likely to lessen when you are able to talk about them. When you don't express them, they accumulate. Present-day disappointments, losses, angers, and fears can become intertwined with old disappointments, losses, angers, and fears, making it difficult to separate old issues from new issues.

- Having a feeling does not mean you need to act on it. How one feels and what one does with those feelings are separate issues.
- View your feelings as a part of you. Let the feelings be your friend, not something that will hurt you.
- Feelings hurt the most when they are denied, minimized, or discounted.
- Feelings aren't there to rule you, but to act as cues and signals.

Family members learn early to quit talking honestly about what is occurring. As one young girl in a substance abusing family said, "In my family we just pretend things are different than they really are." When you feel hopeless and helpless, learning to deny feelings is self-protection and you usually quit talking honestly about feelings early in the denial process.

Experiences can fuel a variety of feelings. You may feel anger, fear, sadness, and embarrassment for lying and making excuses for the addict's out-of-control behavior. You take on false guilt thinking you are responsible for the other person's behavior, you feel guilty for being angry, for having hateful thoughts—"I wish I never married her." "Why can't he just go away and never come back?"

Loneliness is pervasive and a feeling one often finds awkward to own. It is usually not so much a reaction to an event, but a consequence of the inability to be honest about what is happening; the inability to feel heard, respected, and loved by other family members.

Validate that these are common feelings and thoughts. Then lead a discussion by listing feelings on a board. One by one go through each feeling listed, asking each participant if he or she can identify situations where that feeling was experienced, the goal being for each family member to visually see that he or she is not alone in feeling anger, sadness, loneliness, fear, embarrassment, guilt, etc. (If working with an individual family member, instead of using a board, this exercise could be done conversationally.)

If the participants have difficulty identifying feelings, there are common experiences that can serve as examples:

Fear

    My son won't get better, that he will die

    Of a car accident

    Of financial ruin

    I will be left alone

    Of what my husband will say to me, or the kids, or the neighbors

Anger

    For all the excuses

    For the screaming and name-calling

    That he doesn't come home

    That she drives loaded with the kids in the car

    At myself for putting up with this

    He's always asking for money

Sadness

    For not knowing what to do

    For the loneliness I feel

    For watching him self-destruct

    Seeing how her behavior hurts others I love

Guilt

    For screaming at her, calling her names

    For lying to our friends

    For hating someone I'm supposed to love

    For being ashamed of my wife (father, mother, son, etc.)

Embarrassed

    For the scene at school

    For my friends seeing my mother passed out

    When my husband looks at other women the way he does

The handout *Times I Felt* could be an assignment prior to this session, or it could be a warm-up exercise prior to discussion. If used as a warm-up, ask participants to note one example in writing and flush

out additional examples in discussion. Another way to begin a discussion is offering participants the *Feelings Meter* handout.

If time allows, discussion on the belief systems that support or hinder the expression of feelings can be helpful. Otherwise, it may be incorporated into other related sessions.

There are common gender differences in our society as to the expression of feelings—anger is "appropriate" for men but not women; fear and sadness are "appropriate" for women but not men. Ask family members to share early cultural and family messages they received about a specific feeling and feelings in general. The handout *Willingness to Show Feelings* will help them explore this. The handout *Beliefs About Feelings* will allow them to be more specific.

Times I Felt

For each feeling listed, describe three situations in which you felt this way.

Angry

1. _____

_____

2. _____

_____

3. _____

_____

Lonely

1. _____

_____

2. _____

_____

3. _____

_____

Sad

1. _____

_____

2. _____

_____

3. _____

_____

Guilty

1. _____

_____

2. _____

_____

3. _____

_____

Fear

1. _____

_____

2. _____

_____

3. _____

_____

Embarrassed

1. _____

_____

2. _____

_____

3. _____

_____

Love

1. _____

_____

2. _____

_____

3. _____

_____

Feelings Meter

On the meters, mark the levels for the feelings listed as you experience them in your family.

Fear Meter	**Loneliness Meter**	**Guilt Meter**
Very Fearful	Very Lonely	Very Guilty
Fearful	Lonely	Guilty
Somewhat Fearful	Somewhat Lonely	Somewhat Guilty
Rarely Fearful	Rarely Lonely	Rarely Guilty
Never Fearful	Never Lonely	Never Guilty

Sadness Meter	**Embarrassment Meter**	**Anger Meter**
Very Sad	Very Embarrassed	Very Angry
Sad	Embarrassed	Angry
Somewhat Sad	Somewhat Embarrassed	Somewhat Angry
Rarely Sad	Rarely Embarrassed	Rarely Angry
Never Sad	Never Embarrassed	Never Angry

 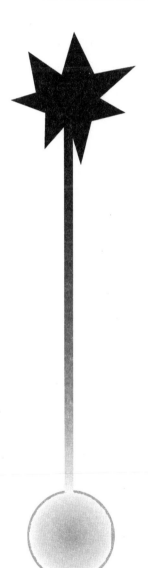 

Willingness to Show Feelings

What are the messages/thoughts that interfere with your willingness to show a specific feeling or feelings in general?

1. _____

_____

2. _____

_____

3. _____

_____

4. _____

_____

Where did you get these messages?

_____

_____

_____

_____

What is the price you pay for holding on to these messages?

_____

_____

_____

_____

Being new at owning your feelings, it will be important for you to know the value of being able to identify and express them.

Some benefits are:

- When I know what my feelings are and I am more honest with myself, I can be more honest with others.
- When I am in touch with my feelings, I will be in a better position to feel close to other people.
- When I know how I feel, I can begin to ask for what I need.
- When I am able to experience feelings, I feel more alive.

List four more reasons it is of value to you to be able to identify and express feelings:

1. _____

_____

2. _____

_____

3. _____

_____

4. _____

_____

Beliefs About Feelings

For each feeling listed, name the beliefs that help you deny (not own) that feeling. Then name the beliefs that support you in the healthy expression of that feeling.

Angry
Examples:

Beliefs that deny or rationalize

I'm out of control if I'm angry.
People won't like me.

_____

_____

_____

_____

Beliefs that support

I get heard.
It's normal to get angry.

_____

_____

_____

_____

Lonely
Examples:

Beliefs that deny or rationalize

It's my fault if I'm lonely.
Something is wrong with me.

_____

_____

_____

_____

Beliefs that support

Everyone gets lonely at times.
Loneliness tells me I need to reach out.

_____

_____

_____

_____

Sad
Examples:

Beliefs that deny or rationalize

No one cares what I feel.
It's just a pity plea.

_____

_____

_____

_____

Beliefs that support

Crying helps me feel better.
Sadness is normal where there is loss.

_____

_____

_____

_____

Guilty
Examples:

Beliefs that deny or rationalize
I can't be strong if I feel guilty.
It's a sign of weakness.

_____

_____

_____

_____

Beliefs that support
Owning guilt is about being accountable.
It allows me to move forward.

_____

_____

_____

_____

Fear
Examples:

Beliefs that deny or rationalize
Someone will take advantage of me.
It means I'm weak.

_____

_____

_____

_____

Beliefs that support
It's natural; it's human.
People can be there for me.

_____

_____

_____

_____

Embarrassed
Examples:

Beliefs that deny or rationalize
I'm never wrong.
I'll look foolish.

_____

_____

_____

_____

Beliefs that support
We all make mistakes.
It happens to everyone at some time.

_____

_____

_____

_____

Love
Examples:

Beliefs that deny or rationalize
No one will love me back.
I'll be vulnerable.

_____

_____

_____

_____

Beliefs that support
It enhances intimacy.
Love is a gift.

_____

_____

_____

_____

Expressing Feelings

Family Objectives

To identify feelings that are easy to express.

To identify feelings that are difficult to express.

Materials Needed

Board

Starting Point

This session is to further the discussion of feelings—specifically, for family members to identify feelings that are easiest to express and feelings that are difficult to express and then to discuss any fears about expressing specific feelings and put those fears into a realistic perspective.

Using a board, list the following feelings:

Anger – Loneliness – Sadness – Guilt – Fear – Embarrassment – Love

Then ask participants:
1. What feelings do you find easiest to express?
2. What feelings do you find difficult to express?
3. What do you fear would happen if you expressed the difficult feelings?

Many times the fear of what will happen if a specific feeling is expressed is rooted in childhood history rather than present day reality. It is helpful to ascertain how realistic the fears are today. If they are realistic, then what needs to occur for the fears to no longer be valid?

Family Strategies

Completing this exercise multi-generationally helps family members recognize familial patterns. Ask participants to answer questions one and two relative to their mothers during their growing-up years and then do the same for their fathers.

Emotional Sociogram

Family Objective

To recognize emotional connections within the family.

Materials Needed

Paper and pens or pencils

Starting Point

Family members need the opportunity to be honest about their emotional connections within the family without having to describe, explain, defend, or rationalize. This exercise helps them break denial about what is being experienced. The exercise is most effective after the sessions of Feelings and Expressing Feelings have been conducted.

Ask family members to draw a large circle and place themselves in the center of the circle. Then ask them to position each individual family member in the circle in relation to the emotional closeness to his- or herself. Once all family members have been positioned, have them go back and note the predominant feelings associated with each member.

After all participants have finished, have each one share what they noted. The focus of this discussion can be centered on how they would like the connections to be different and what needs to occur for that to happen.

Examples:

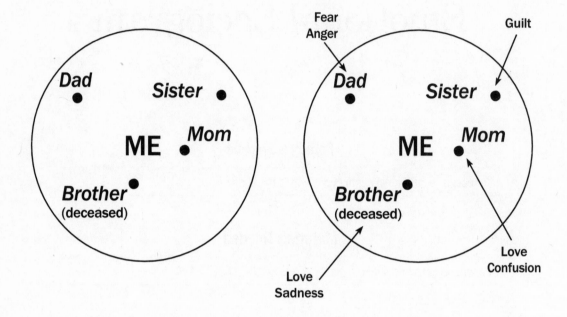

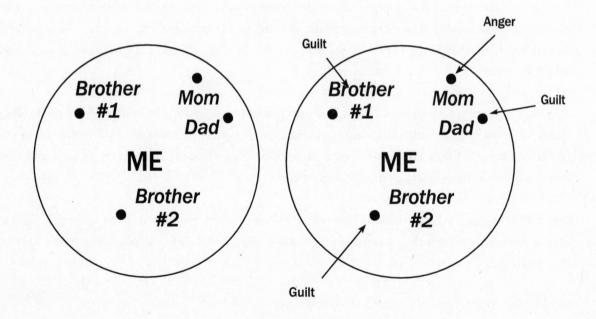

Portrait of Feelings

Family Objectives

To express feelings.

To express one's relationship to feelings.

Materials Needed

Collage materials for each participant:

3 to 5 magazines (nearly any magazine can be used; it is suggested that there be an assortment)

14" x 17" pieces of paper, scotch tape, scissors

Starting Point

In addictive family systems, feelings are often something to be feared or avoided. It is natural for family members to find ways to defend against their feelings. Ultimately, this interferes with the ability to express feelings. Artwork can be a wonderful form of expression. It takes away the defense of words, allows the unconscious to be more accessible and if participants let go of perfectionism it can be fun. Depending on the feelings you want family members to explore, ask them to draw a picture or create a collage to represent past and present experiences.

A collage is made by taking pictures, words, and/or letters from magazines to make a statement. Depending on time, offer participants twenty to thirty minutes to create their collages. Suggest they begin their collages by flipping through a magazine and being open and receptive to what they see rather than looking for specific words or pictures.

Examples:

Picture of Sadness

1) A smiling person may represent what you did to mask your sadness as a child.
2) The word "blue" may describe a color tone to your sadness.
3) A cloud may represent an intense amount of sadness and tears within you.
4) A woman may represent your mother, who reminds you of your greatest source of sadness.

Picture of Anger

1) A volcano may represent how explosive and frightening you perceive your anger.
2) A bottle of alcohol may represent that you often drink to get rid of your anger.
3) A dog may represent being mad at your dad for giving your dog away when you were a kid.
4) A car may represent a form of escape when you're angry.

Picture of Fear

1) A person of the opposite sex may represent that you are afraid of the opposite sex.
2) The word "no" may represent how difficult you find it to say no.
3) A hand may represent getting hit.
4) A cartoon showing a person walking on a tightrope may represent how fearful life is for you.

Picture of Guilt

1) A person eating sweets may represent what you do with guilt.
2) A child in leg braces may represent believing you are somehow responsible for this birth defect.
3) A bottle of liquor may represent tremendous guilt related to addiction.
4) A car racing down the road may symbolically represent trying to make up for your inadequacies, your guilt.

Picture of Happiness

1) A picture of the forest may remind you of the feelings of peace and solitude you felt walking through the forest as a teenager.
2) A group of people all singing together may represent a feeling of belonging that you experience with certain friends (it doesn't literally have to have anything to do with singing).
3) A family in a car may represent a memory of a fun family time.
4) Books may represent the good feeling you experience when you are involved in learning something.

Remind participants these are their collages. Only they will interpret the pictures and/or words. There is no right or wrong way to complete a collage.

Anger

Family Objectives

To recognize different expressions of anger.

To identify core beliefs that sabotage healthy expressions of anger.

Materials Needed

Handout – Anger Meter

Starting Point

Anger is one of the most pervasive and distorted feelings in families affected by addiction. This session offers family members an opportunity to focus specifically on acknowledging their anger and the many ways they distort it.

Didactic

In families affected by addiction, anger is one of the most distorted feelings. Family members are usually anger avoidant and go to great lengths to deny it, or they are chronically angry and/or rageful. They may be frightened of their own anger; they may be frightened of other people's anger; or they may have so much anger that they feel explosive. Family members may have diverse experiences with the expression of their own anger or that of others.

Unhealthy anger can present itself in many ways.
1) Anger can be overtly expressed—yelling, shaming statements.
2) Anger can be covertly expressed. Anger expressed covertly is passive-aggressive in nature. Passive-aggressive behavior is often known as "sideways" anger because rather than being

expressed directly, it comes out sideways at a person or in a specific situation. It may involve procrastination, being late, and the use of sarcasm and demeaning comments toward others. Family members who have unresolved issues between one another often make fun of each other. While on the surface the content may be delivered in a joking manner, underneath is anger.

3) Another form of anger is retaliatory anger. When a family member finds a way to settle the score, having kept a mental log of who has wronged him or her, then seeks ways to get even.

4) Anger can be masked as isolation. "I don't need help from anyone." The angry person does not need anything from anybody at any time.

5) Anger is also manifested as depression. Unresolved grief, pain, shame, trauma, and abuse issues can result in tremendous anger, which turned inward is depression. It is much safer and more socially acceptable to present a depressed mood to society than an angry mood.

For many of you, anger avoidance is a key issue. You may have learned from a very early age that you need to quickly diffuse your anger to avoid possible negative consequences. With this model internalized, as adults you avoid anger to keep yourself safe. You may hold a variety of personal beliefs that preclude you from expressing anger. These may include: I am ashamed of myself if I am angry; if I express my anger I will be shamed and blamed by others; being angry means losing control.

Anger, which is a feeling, can transform into rage, which is a behavior. Often, family members in early recovery say if they get in touch with their anger, they will "lose it." It is important to ask them what they mean by "to lose it." Does it mean raising their voice, calling someone names, hitting someone, or hurting themselves? Family members' fears of what would happen should they express their anger are usually far worse than the reality of what would occur. They need to identify their fears to be able to put them into a realistic perspective.

Share with family members that anger is a healthy human feeling that can mobilize and energize. Like all feelings, anger is a cue, a signal that needs to be honored and listened to. Anger indicates there is a problem or a need that is unaddressed. There are choices as to what to do with it, how to express it, and when to express it.

Dialogue with family members about what they think they do with their anger. Offer them the handout *Anger Meter* and allow ten minutes for them to complete it and then discuss.

Optional: Ask participants to create a collage related to their relationship with anger. (See *Portrait of Feelings* session for examples.)

Anger Meter

Mark your level of anger on the meter below.

In general, I consider myself

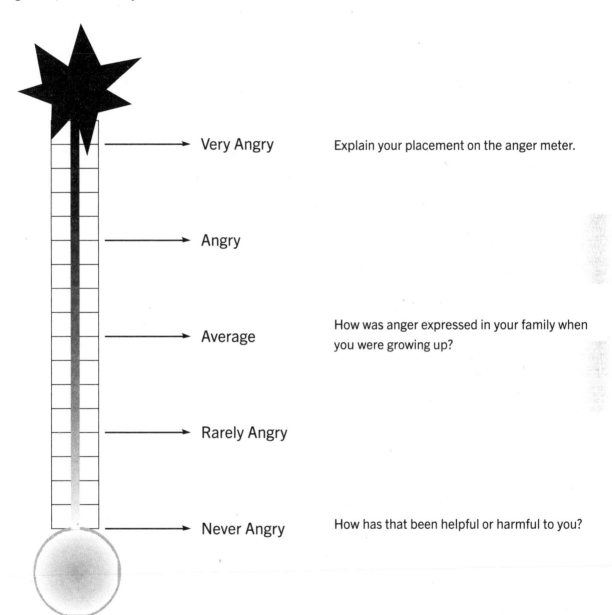

→ Very Angry   Explain your placement on the anger meter.

→ Angry

→ Average   How was anger expressed in your family when you were growing up?

→ Rarely Angry

→ Never Angry   How has that been helpful or harmful to you?

Resentments

To explore the issue of resentments.

Materials Needed

Board

Starting Point

Resentments are like burrs in a saddle blanket: if you do not get rid of them they can fester and grow into an infection. Resentments often stem from unrealistic expectations or distorted thinking and are experienced when someone is feeling discounted, slighted, or unheard. Ask family members to show with hands how many identify with carrying resentments. Have them identify resentments they are carrying. List those on the board. If they have difficulty identifying resentments, use either of the following sentence stems to become focused.

> I resent . . .
> I am resentful that . . .

Examples might be:

> I resent that I have to be in this group.
> I resent it when my wife tells me I remind her of her first husband.
> I resent it when my son doesn't call me except when he needs money.

From the board, take one example, and explore ways to move from that place of resentment. One of the ways to move from resentment is to ask what is the resentment covering? Is it covering up another feeling? Such as, "resenting being in this group" may more honestly be stated as "I am afraid of some of my feelings that may surface in these sessions."

Another way to move from resentment is to say what you need or what you would like. The resentment about being compared to a previous spouse could be stated, "I need you to tell me what it is you are asking of me when you are upset." Resentment about always being called for money becomes "I'd like you to call so we can talk, but don't ask for money again."

Appropriate sentence stems are:

> I resent it when . . .
> I resent that . . .
> I need . . .
> I want . . .
> I prefer . . .
> I would like . . .

If a family member's resentments are about feeling "less than," then refer to the session about *Shame Attacks*. Resenting others is often about control—resenting those who you believe will interfere with your plans. If this is so, refer back to the session on Giving Up Control.

Explain that different ways to move away from a place of resentment are:

1. Identify and own the feelings the resentment is covering.
2. State what you need, want, prefer.
3. When assuming, check the assumption.
4. Put yourself in somebody else's shoes; it may allow your expectations to be more realistic.
5. Be willing to live and let live.

On a daily basis, until the next session, ask the participants to make a list of the little or big things that throughout each day they find themselves feeling resentment about. In the next session explore what they can do about their resentments.

The following imagery is a helpful exercise to close the session.

Imagery Direction

When asking people to participate in an imagery, begin by acknowledging that it may feel awkward in the beginning, but that it can be highly valuable if they allow themselves to relax and be open to the process.

It is suggested you have soft music playing in the background. The key is for the presenter to talk slowly, and allow the participants time to breathe deeply, to hear the words, to be with the words. It is not necessary to have a discussion about the imagery once completed. In fact, that is often contraindicated because it moves the participant from an emotional/spiritual experience into an intellectual realm.

Begin the experience by asking the participants to find a comfortable sitting position, uncross their arms and legs, and begin to take slow deep breaths. As you offer these directions, begin to pace your speaking so that it is soothing and relaxing.

Letting Go of Resentments Imagery

Sit down in a quiet, comfortable place. Uncross your arms and legs and gently close your eyes. Slowly take several deep breaths. As you breathe in, visualize warm and healing energy coming into your body. As you breathe out, imagine stress and tension slowly leaving your body.

As you continue to breathe deeply, become aware of your feet on the floor. Gently move them around and feel the connection between your body and the earth. Visualize your connection with the earth and slowly breathe in and out. Allow any stress and tension to melt away.

Breathe in . . . breathe out. Breathe in . . . breathe out.

Slowly become aware of your legs. Breathe healing energy into your legs and feel the safety and warmth of the healing energy. Slowly feel the energy as it moves up from your legs to your waist and into your back. Allow the muscles in your legs, waist, chest, and back to relax as your body floats freely.

Breathe in . . . and out. Breathe in . . . and out.

Feel your arms and shoulders loosen as the stress leaves them and the healing energy penetrates to your deepest muscles. Allow your neck and throat to relax as you continue to breathe in warm and healing energy. Feel your facial muscles soften and smooth out against the bones. Become aware of the beat of your heart. Feel your connection to your Higher Power.

Take a deep breath in . . . and out. Take a deep breath in . . . and out. Take a deep breath in . . . and out.

Say to yourself—

> *Today I let go of my expectations.*
> *Today I let go of my expectations.*
> *Today I let go of my fears.*
> *Today I let go of my fears.*

Visualize your Higher Power who loves you unconditionally and guides your journey in recovery. Visualize your Higher Power protecting you and keeping you safe. Visualize your body and spirit being surrounded by healing energy.

Continue to breathe in . . . and out. Breathe in . . . and out.

Scan through your body and slowly become aware of where in your body you may be holding your resentments. Feel that place in your body. Slowly breathe healing energy into that place.

As you continue to breathe, say to yourself,

> *Today I release my resentments. They no longer serve me.*
> *Today I release my resentments. They no longer serve me.*

Slowly visualize your resentments beginning to leave your body. Feel your resentments floating away from your body. Continue to breathe in healing energy. Feel your resentments float away.

Say to yourself—

> *Today I release my need for control. It no longer serves me.*
> *Today acceptance is the answer to all my problems.*
> *Today I know that my Higher Power guides my journey in recovery.*
> *Today I choose to have a spiritual connection with myself.*
> *Today I choose to have a spiritual connection with my Higher Power.*
> *Today I choose serenity over the chaos of my family's addiction.*
> *Today I choose to live life guided by my Higher Power.*

Take a few moments to gently float and allow yourself to feel the power of these words. You no longer need to hold on to resentments, fears, and the need to control. You can now live a life filled with hope, a life of serenity.

As you continue to breathe, slowly and deeply, become aware of your body in this room. Become aware of your head . . . your neck . . . your shoulders and arms. Become aware of your chest . . . back . . . your waist . . . your legs . . . your feet. Become aware of your connection to the earth. Gently begin to shift your body around and when you are ready, open your eyes.

Remember this imagery was to help you release expectations and resentments. Each day as you learn to release expectations, fears, and resentments, you learn to live life guided by your Higher Power.

Sadness

Family Objectives

To identify core beliefs that sabotage healthy expressions of sadness.

To recognize that releasing sadness can empower recovery.

Materials Needed

Handout – Sadness Meter

Starting Point

Where there is loss there is sadness, and where there is sadness there may be tears. It is not unusual when working with people who have experienced difficult and painful experiences that they have not cried in a long time. When that is true, sometimes it's because of the fear that no one will be there to offer comfort or that crying will be perceived as being weak or vulnerable. The fears of what would happen should they cry is usually far worse than the reality of what actually does occur. While there are significant gender differences in expressing sadness/pain/loss—men having greater difficulty than women—both men and women may learn to defend against their sadness.

Dialogue with family members about what they think they do with their sadness. Offer them the handout *Sadness Meter* and allow ten minutes for them to complete it, then discuss.

Optional: Ask participants to create a collage related to their relationship with sadness. (See *Portrait of Feelings* session for examples.)

Conclude the session with the following imagery.

Imagery Direction

When asking people to participate in an imagery, begin by acknowledging that it may feel awkward in the beginning, but that it can be highly valuable if they allow themselves to relax and be open to the process.

It is suggested you have soft music playing in the background. The key is for the presenter to talk slowly and allow the participants time to breathe deeply, to hear the words, and to be with the words. It is not necessary to have a discussion about the imagery once completed. In fact, that is often contraindicated because it moves the participant from an emotional/spiritual experience into an intellectual realm.

Begin the experience by asking the participants to find a comfortable sitting position, uncross their arms and legs, and begin to take slow deep breaths in and out. As you offer these directions, begin to pace your speaking so that it is soothing and relaxing.

Letting Go of the Pain of Grief Imagery

Uncross your arms and legs and sit comfortably. Take a deep breath in and out. Now more slowly. In . . . and out. When you are ready, gently close your eyes. Begin to breathe into the areas of your body that hold your feelings.

As you breathe in, visualize healing energy flowing into those areas where you are holding your feelings. Visualize your Higher Power moving into that place where you have held your pain, your hurt, your anger, and your abandonment. Visualize your Higher Power nurturing your scared inner child. You are safe here. No one can hurt you now. It is safe to let these feelings out.

Repeat after me—
> *I don't want to hold on to these feelings anymore.*
> *I release them. They are not mine to carry anymore.*
> *I don't want to hold on to these feelings anymore.*
> *I release them. They are not mine to carry anymore.*

Continue to breathe light and energy into that place of hurt and pain. Begin to feel the tension . . . the pain . . . leave your body.

Say to yourself—

> *I will not hold onto this energy anymore.*
>
> *It's not mine now.*
>
> *I release this energy.*
>
> *I will not carry these feelings any longer.*
>
> *I acknowledge my loss. I can feel my feelings.*
>
> *I know that no amount of bargaining or manipulation will restore my loss.*
>
> *I have a willingness to move on.*
>
> *I have a willingness to withdraw my emotional investment in that which has been lost.*
>
> *I am a powerful person in recovery.*

As you continue to breathe deeply, visualize all the pain of your grief leaving your body. Visualize your body being replenished with light and love from your Higher Power. Visualize your body safe here in this room. When you are ready, you may open your eyes.

Sadness Meter

Mark your level of sadness on the meter below:

In general, I consider myself

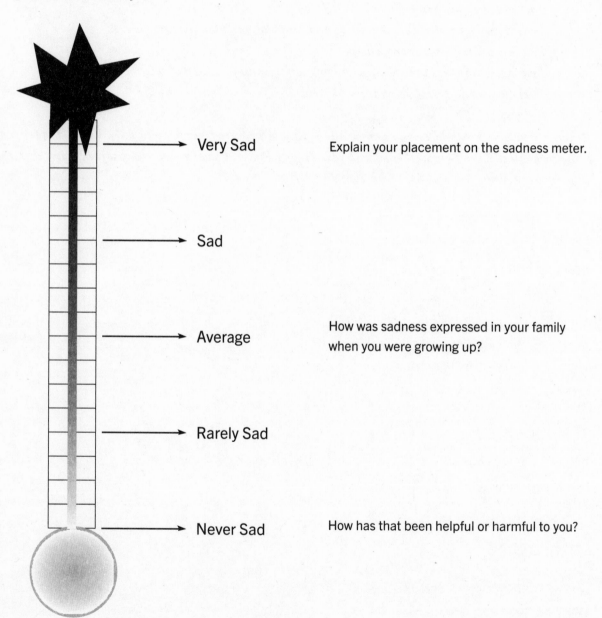

Very Sad

Explain your placement on the sadness meter.

Sad

Average

How was sadness expressed in your family when you were growing up?

Rarely Sad

Never Sad

How has that been helpful or harmful to you?

Toxic Shame

Family Objective

To recognize shame-based messages.

Materials Needed

Handout – Shaming Messages

Starting Point

In working with the family it is critical to address the internalized shame that pervades the addicted person and family members. It is vital that they separate behavior from their personal worth and value. Define the term *shame* and explain how it is learned. Then give participants the opportunity to identify their own perpetuation of shame-based beliefs and how to employ a stop technique.

Didactic

Shame is the belief that there is something wrong with you. For some it is the painful feeling that comes from the belief that there is something inherently wrong with who they are, while for many others the more they know their shame, the more they disconnect from their feelings. Words that are reflective of shame are—bad, inadequate, ugly, stupid, incompetent, less than, inferior, dirty, damaged, or damaged goods.

To live with shame is to feel alienated and defeated, never quite good enough to belong. Shame is an isolating experience that makes you think and feel completely alone and intensely and profoundly unlovable. Shame is about personal worth and value, a matter of identity, not about behavior. In addition to feeling defective, shame makes you feel that others can see through you and into your defectiveness. You feel exposed.

Guilt is when you make a mistake. Shame is when you believe you are the mistake.

Ask participants to think of examples of shaming messages they heard when they were growing up, such as "You are so stupid" or "Can't you get anything right?" Then ask them to identify shaming behaviors they experienced, such as parents yelling at them in front of friends or mocking them for their sexuality. If one was raised in an environment where shame was internalized, it is easier to continue to take on shame than to reject it, especially if today as an adult, there is an offender in the family. Many spouses, partners, and/or parents of an addicted person take on shame from the addict who may rage, name call, or behave in embarrassing and hurtful ways. Lead a discussion into how shaming messages and/or behaviors are present in their life and impacting them today. Do they yell at their own children in public? Do they tell others they are stupid? Are they afraid to try new things for fear they will make a mistake? Do they think of others as smarter than they are?

As a shame reduction exercise, you can offer participants the handout *Shaming Messages* and then discuss or lead a discussion around the questions without the handout.

Because you often do to others what has been done to you, it is likely that if you were shamed as a child or young adult you are shaming yourself now. A shame-producing statement is one that only causes you to feel poorly about yourself. These kinds of statements often begin with "I am just so . . ." or "The trouble with me is . . ." or "What I really don't like about myself is . . ." When said in disgust, these types of statements are shame producing. Shame-based statements are also stated as if they are absolutes, non-negotiable facts, never to be challenged or changed.

Take participants through the following shame reduction exercise:
1. What is a shame-based statement that you make to yourself?
2. Where does it come from? Unhealthy shame is learned from past experiences. One is not born with toxic shame. By asking the question—"Where does it come from"—you are planting the seed that it comes from outside of them. You are looking for a generic response

to the question, such as it came from my father, my mother, the boarding school I was raised in, the music I listened to, etc.

3. Give an example of a time or situation in which the statement was false, a time the statement was just "not quite so true." Examples: Someone says, "I don't have an artistic bone in my body." They counter it with, "I put a project together and the colors came together nicely. It wasn't a piece of art, but it was okay." Or someone says, "I don't have a brain in my head." Counter it with, "But I was on a committee one time and contributed a good idea. It wasn't something that changed the world; it was just a good idea." Or, "I'm a lousy parent." Countered with, "I'm in family counseling and I'm learning how to better the situation."

You are trying to bring to participants an awareness of shame-based statements by helping them identify the language so that when they do make such a statement they can apply a STOP technique and ask, "Where does that come from?" and then give themselves an example of it not being true.

If participants do this repetitively, it can change their shame-based thinking to esteem-building thoughts.

You may want to conclude the session with the following affirmations imagery.

Imagery Direction

When asking people to participate in an imagery, begin by acknowledging that it may feel awkward in the beginning, but that it can be highly valuable if they allow themselves to relax and be open to the process.

It is suggested you have soft music playing in the background. The key is for the presenter to talk slowly, and allow the participants time to breathe deeply, to hear the words, and to be with the words. It is not necessary to have a discussion about the imagery once completed. In fact, that is often contraindicated because it moves the participant from an emotional/spiritual experience into an intellectual realm.

Begin the experience by asking the participants to find a comfortable sitting position, uncross their arms and legs, and begin to take slow deep breaths in and out. As you offer these directions, begin to pace your speaking so that it is soothing and relaxing.

Affirmation Imagery

Find a comfortable position and uncross your arms and legs. Take a deep breath in . . . and out. Take another deep breath in . . . and out. If you haven't already done so, gently close your eyes.

As you breathe slowly and deeply, begin to relax your body, allowing the tension to dissolve . . . the worries of the day, the stresses of decisions moving out of your body.

Take a deep breath in . . . and out.

If there are any places in your body that still feel tight or tense, where you are holding energy you don't need . . . put your awareness into those places . . . breathe into them. As you breathe out, imagine the tension or the excess energy releasing and dissolving away so that your entire body feels deeply relaxed.

Slowly, breathe in . . . and out.

Think of a place you can go in your mind . . . a magical place . . . a special place just for you. Now take yourself to that place. For some it is a pond out in the woods . . . for others it is a rock perched on the sand at the beach . . . or it may be your own home. Wherever it is, it is your place. Go there now.

You may have friends with you . . . you may have family . . . or you may choose to be with yourself. This is your time . . . your moment . . . this is your choice.

With your eyes closed, you slowly become engulfed in waves of color. Pinks . . . blues . . . greens . . . whites . . . purples . . . oranges. Colors of love . . . colors of safety . . . colors of nurturance. These colors may be soft, pastel, rich, and intense. Whatever the colors, they feel loving and safe.

Continue to breathe deeply . . . in . . . and out.

Now, in your very special place full of very loving, safe colors, be with these words:
> *I am very special.*
> *I may never have had the opportunity to believe in my specialness.*
> *I may believe in it today.*
> *I no longer deserve to live my life in fear.*
> *I trust in myself. My perceptions are far more accurate than I have been willing to believe.*
> *Today, I may respond with the vulnerability of my inner child and the strength of my adult being.*

Feelings are to be listened to; they are cues and signals that indicate where I am and what I need.

Mistakes are a sign of growing. I will be gentle with myself.

Being less than perfect makes me human.

Success is not relative to others. Success is a feeling of love and accomplishment for myself.

Recovery is accepting myself for who I am, not waiting for others to define or approve of me.

It is safe to take time to play today. Play fuels my creativity, tickles my inner child, and nurtures my soul.

In faith, I find the strength to survive times of great fear and sadness.

I surround myself with people who respect me and treat me well.

Be with those words, in your magical place of color. Know that you may return to this place any time you choose. Take a slow deep breath in . . . and out. When you are ready, you may open your eyes.

SHAMING MESSAGES

1. Give examples of shaming messages you experienced while growing up and/or as an adult.

    You're stupid, dumb, ugly. You'll never be successful.

    _____

    _____

    _____

2. Give examples of shaming behaviors you experienced while growing up and/or as an adult.

    Parents yelled at you in a public place; you were criticized in front of coworkers.

    _____

    _____

    _____

3. Give examples of how you see those shaming messages/behaviors present in your life today.

    Yelling at my own children in a public place; telling others they are stupid and incompetent; being afraid of making a mistake; thinking others are smarter than I am; not trying things I'd like to do.

    _____

    _____

    _____

Shame Attacks

Family Objectives

To understand shame attacks.

To learn to stop the shame attack and move to healthier thinking.

Materials Needed

Handout — Recovery from Shame Attacks

Starting Point

It is important that this session follow the previous one on Toxic Shame as it will help family members recognize when they experience a shame attack and how to stop it and move to healthier thinking.

Didactic

When you grow up in a dysfunctional environment filled with shaming messages and behaviors, your core belief that you are flawed is ever present. So, when in stressful situations or when someone displays shaming behavior toward you or gives a shaming message, you may experience what is called a Shame Attack. You may also experience a Shame Attack based on your perception of a person or situation. A Shame Attack occurs when your internal beliefs that you are flawed, stupid, ugly, or incompetent are re-engaged. You often feel like a young child again, defenseless, abandoned, terrified of this person or situation because it recreates the trauma you experienced in earlier environments.

Shame Attacks incorporate all-or-nothing thinking. An example of a Shame Attack is:

"I made a mistake in my finances and I bounced a check. Since I bounced this check, I'll probably bounce many more, I will have to declare bankruptcy, and then my credit will be ruined." From here, it's then very easy to start to shame yourself by saying, "I really am stupid and I can't do anything right."

Another example of a Shame Attack is:

You are expected to present the culmination of a project at work tomorrow. You have worked diligently but today you heard a coworker's presentation and suddenly you know you will look unprepared and stupid. You immediately "catastrophize" the situation, saying to yourself, "I will lose my job. They will be sorry they hired me," and on and on.

Ask participants if they can identify with the concept of a Shame Attack and to give examples.

In recovery, it is extremely important to learn how to get out of a Shame Attack. If you are experiencing a Shame Attack, you need to:
- *Identify it for what it is.*
  This is a Shame Attack. I am feeling less than, and catastrophizing (only seeing the worst).
- *Stop the thinking.*
- *Check the reality.*

Look at the previous two examples. What is the reality here?

Check-bouncing situation

> *Reality:* you bounced a check. You made an error in your arithmetic. You were stressed and weren't thinking when you wrote the check. Most people will occasionally bounce a check. You can call the payee the check was made to and tell him or her of your plan for repayment.

Fear of presenting work project

> *Reality:* you feel insecure. Another person made a good presentation. You have worked hard on this but are anxious. You want your supervisor to be impressed. None of this means you are incompetent. It says you are anxious. Past experience indicates your confidence shows once you begin your presentation.

- *Get outside feedback.*
  In a Shame Attack you are distorting the reality. You have lost sight of what is real and true and revert to fear.
- *Look at the origin of the shaming statement.*
  This is another important long-term tool in stopping a Shame Attack. After you've garnered a more realistic perspective, ask yourself, "What were the harsh words I used against myself?" They were usually words such as "I am stupid." "I can't do anything right." When did you first come to believe those messages about yourself?

In the previous session on Toxic Shame, participants were encouraged to note self-deprecating statements they made throughout the day. When they spoke harshly to themselves, they were perpetuating a Shame Attack. Take a few examples from participants and with each message they gave themselves, ask them to stop and reflect on where that message came from.

Example:

"I'm so stupid I can't get anything right."
Stop: Where did you first hear that?
Answer: My dad.

Now direct participants to give an example of their statement not being true, the purpose being to get them out of an all-or-nothing shaming statement.

Example:

"I'll never amount to anything."
Stop: Where did you first hear that?
Answer: My mother.
Example of this not being true: I now own my own business.

In a Shame Attack, you may feel the vulnerability of a child, often because you were shamed at a young age when indeed you were vulnerable. So when in an attack, talk yourself into your stronger adult reality.

These statements come from outside of you. You were not born with shaming messages or toxic shame; they had to be given to you. You were told these things by your parents, caregivers, relatives, or spouse or partner. So when experiencing a Shame Attack, you need to recognize that the message comes from outside of yourself.

Offer the handout *Recovery from Shame Attacks* for participants to use as a tool for stopping Shame Attacks.

Recovery from Shame Attacks

- *Identify it for what it is.*
  This is a Shame Attack. I am feeling less than . . . and catastrophizing (only seeing the worst).

- *Stop the thinking.*

- *Check the reality.*

  Check bouncing situation.
  Reality: you bounced a check. You made an error in your arithmetic. You were stressed and weren't thinking when you wrote the check.
  Reality: most people will bounce a check sometime.
  Reality: you can call the payee the check was made to and tell them of your plan for repayment.

  Fear of presenting work project.
  Reality: you feel insecure. Another person made a good presentation. You have worked hard on this but are anxious. You want your superior to be impressed. None of this means you are incompetent. It says you are anxious. Past experience says your confidence shows once you begin your presentation.

- *Get outside feedback.*
  In a Shame Attack you are distorting the reality. You have lost sight of what is real and true and revert to fear.

- *Look at the origin of the shaming statement.*
  This is another important long-term tool in stopping a Shame Attack. After you've garnered a more realistic perspective, ask yourself: What were the harsh words I used against myself? They are usually words such as "I am stupid." "I can't do anything right." When did you first come to believe those messages about yourself?

Walking the Path of Recovery

Overview

This section concludes *Family Strategies*. Several of these sessions can easily be incorporated into the therapeutic process prior to the closing phase. They were included in this final section because the issues addressed are those that family members can best explore and discuss only after many of the other sessions are completed. The last three sessions offer a closing to the family treatment process.

Spirituality gives family members an opportunity to explore their relationship or lack of relationship with a Higher Power and consider its role in their recovery.

Spiritual Journey creates the opportunity for family members to identify the meaning and practice of a spiritual path in recovery.

Forgiveness is a session that may occur spontaneously during the treatment process. It offers family members a way to talk about their thoughts and feelings about forgiveness. For many, to forgive or not forgive may be a bypass to addressing other more difficult feelings.

Assertive Rights reinforces each family member's personal rights. This session could easily be spontaneously incorporated into the treatment process at the facilitator's discretion. It was placed here to behaviorally reinforce family members' recovery goals.

Family Meetings creates a format for family rituals that will support the family in future dialogue. This session aids in developing family cohesiveness and healthy communication. This format can be used with couples, large family units, and families with children at home or of adult age.

Portrait of Recovery allows each family member to concretize his or her recovery plan and take steps to make it more obtainable.

Recovery Plan is a format for 1) identifying codependent behaviors family members want to avoid; 2) identifying behaviors that are triggers for relapse to codependent behaviors; and 3) identifying specific recovery behaviors.

Closing Ritual offers a healthy closing to the family treatment process through the use of imageries, affirmations, and/or the presentation of a tangible object.

Spirituality

Family Objective

To explore the role of spirituality in the recovery process.

Starting Point

Many people will create personal changes predominantly from a cognitive behavioral model. Others will utilize spiritual practices and religious faith. By the time the addicted person and family members seek help they often feel spiritually bankrupt and disconnected from, or even angry with their Higher Power or God. It is important to explore how spiritual practice or religious beliefs may hinder their willingness to engage in new ways of relating to their family and themselves and to offer them a framework for the role of spirituality in their healing process. Explore with participants the role of religion or spirituality in their lives.

Questions to explore with them are:
1. As a child, were you forced to attend church (synagogue) or to otherwise participate in religious practices?
2. If your involvement in your church or synagogue ended, what made you stop?
3. If you didn't attend any type of church, how was that decision made?
4. If you were involved in a church or a religious group, describe your experience. Fun? Scary? Boring? Hopeful? Meaningful? Other?
5. Was there contradiction between your religious teachings and what occurred in your daily life? In many families children lived a contradiction between the religious teachings they were taught and what happened in their daily lives. Instead of respect, did you hear verbal abuse? Instead of loving behavior, did you see one parent cause another intense anger or sadness? Instead of honesty, did you witness your parents lying? Were you ever told to lie for a family member under the guise of "protection?" How many times did you return home from church to neglect, abuse, or addiction kept hidden from the outside world?

187

6. Were there any particular rituals or ceremonies that you especially valued or that held significance for you? What were they?
7. Today, looking back on your early religious experiences, what positive influences are still with you? Are there any negative influences still with you?

After discussing these questions with participants, introduce the many concepts of recovery that are spiritually based.

Didactic

You embark on a spiritual path when you let go of your fears and defenses and allow yourself to hear the truth. Realizing your fallibility and accepting responsibility for making choices is a spiritual process. Accepting the imperfections that lay at the core of your being and granting yourself permission to be the imperfect human being that you are allows you to let others be who they are. Spirituality is grounded in the acceptance of the awareness, "I am not in control." Sheldon Kopp, author of *If You Meet the Buddha on the Road, Kill Him*, wrote, "No matter how well we may prepare, the moment belongs to God."

Accepting what you cannot control does not mean giving up all efforts to have order in your life. It does not mean you have to thrive in chaos. It means you give up the illusion that you can control what no one can. In accepting that which you cannot control, you give up needlessly trying. You are powerless over people, places, and things, not your recovery. In Twelve Step programs they have a saying: "Surrender to win."

Spirituality is a surrendering process: surrendering the illusion that you must have all the answers and must be in charge so you can hide your shame. You surrender to your inability to change the past and to your powerlessness to control the future. Living in the here and now is a fundamental spiritual concept.

Spiritual development comes with spiritual practice, just as the person who wants to be physically fit must exercise. Without the workouts—nothing happens. If you set your course toward inner calm and peace of mind, daily spiritual practice is necessary.

To grow spiritually you must "walk the walk." Practicing spirituality means that you:
*   Be present, be in the here and now
*   Stay attuned to inner guidance
*   Be authentic

- Put forth the effort
- Let go of the attachment to the results
- Believe in divine guidance and the choice it offers

Ask participants to give examples of how they have or have not "walked the walk." For the participants who believe they identify with a spiritual program, a solid explanation of naming how they walk their spiritual path can reinforce their spiritual practices.

Spirituality is a process of turning inward to the part of you that is connected to the larger context. Some spiritual practices to connect with your inner life are:

- Prayer
- Meditation
- Silence/quietness
- Guided imagery
- Living a "thought"-full life

Many people include deep breathing and relaxation in their rituals. By definition, spirituality derives from the Latin word *spiritus*, which means "the act of breathing." Breathing allows one to be within his/her own body, to go "inside."

Prayer is common in church, at ashram, or temple. It is also an important part of spiritual practice throughout the day. Some people have a favorite meditation book and read from it during times of prayer. Some people get on their knees; others have a sitting area where they are surrounded by favorite objects, photographs, and plants. Prayer and/or meditation is something one can do while sitting in the living room, lying in bed, walking along the beach, or jogging in the park. Both prayer and meditation are practices that nurture and develop a connection to self and spirit. Prayer is an act that puts one in touch with a power greater than all else.

Discuss these points by asking participants to identify and examine their spiritual priorities. For those who desire, conclude the discussion with focus on specific plans for greater spiritual practice.

Spiritual Journey

Family Objective

To discuss and understand the spiritual journey of the Twelve Steps.

Materials Needed

Handout – Spiritual Pathway Board

Starting Point

Discuss the following material about the spiritual journey.

Didactic

Spiritual growth is a journey that continues throughout our lifetime. When our spiritual life is out of balance, everything is out of balance. A belief in a Higher Power rarely comes instantly. It does not strike like a lightning bolt. Faith is acquired through one's daily activities.

On a board write out Step Two from the Twelve Steps of Alcoholics Anonymous:
"Came to believe that a Power greater than ourselves could restore us to sanity."

Then offer participants this version for discussion.

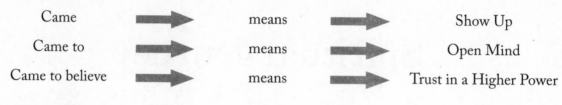

Came	→	means	→	Show Up
Came to	→	means	→	Open Mind
Came to believe	→	means	→	Trust in a Higher Power

Step Two is achieved by taking small calming steps on an enlightening journey. The journey does not lead to a destination or end point called spiritual life. Rather, there are many spiritual rewards along the pathway. The payoff comes in making the journey, not reaching a destination.

Give participants the handout *Spiritual Pathway*. When complete, discuss the phrases that describe their spiritual path and what blocks them from this path.

Read the following, "Footprints," and discuss.

One night I dreamed a dream. As I was walking along the beach with my Lord. Across the dark sky flashed scenes from my life. For each scene, I noticed two sets of footprints in the sand, one belonging to me and one to my Lord.

After the last scene of my life flashed before me, I looked back at the footprints in the sand and to my surprise I noticed that many times along the path of my life, especially at the very lowest and saddest times, there was only one set of footprints.

This always bothered me and I questioned the Lord about my dilemma. "Lord, you told me when I decided to follow you, you would walk and talk with me all the way. But I'm aware that during the most troublesome times of my life there is only one set of footprints. I just don't understand why, when I needed you most, you leave me."

He whispered, "My precious child, I love you and I will never leave you, never, ever, during your trials and testing. When you saw only one set of footprints, it was then that I carried you."

© 1964 Margaret Fishback Powers

The following imagery offers closure for the session. This imagery is meant as a guide for participants to begin to visualize their own spirituality.

Imagery Direction

When asking people to participate in an imagery, begin by acknowledging that it may feel awkward at first, but that it can be highly valuable if they allow themselves to relax and be open to the process.

It is suggested you have soft music playing in the background. The key is for the presenter to talk slowly, and allow the participants time to breathe deeply, to hear the words, to be with the words. It is not necessary to have a discussion about the imagery once completed. In fact, that is often contraindicated because it moves the participant from an emotional/spiritual experience into an intellectual realm.

Begin the experience by asking the participants to find a comfortable sitting position, uncross their arms and legs, and begin to take slow deep breaths in and out. As you offer these directions, begin to pace your speaking so that it is soothing and relaxing.

Connecting to a Higher Power Imagery

The purpose of this meditation is to develop a spiritual connection with yourself and your Higher Power. To walk the road of recovery requires patience and dedication to your spiritual program. It is important as you continue on your recovery journey to develop your spiritual connection on a daily basis. Many in recovery do this through prayer and meditation.

There are many wonderful books of daily meditations that you may find useful. Some participants in recovery create their own meditations and prayers. They usually involve visualizing one's own Higher Power and also visualizing soothing and spiritual places.

Gently sit back and close your eyes. Begin to breathe slowly and deeply. Focus on your breathing.

Take a deep breath in . . . and out. Take a deep breath in . . . and out.

As you breathe in, visualize your Higher Power filling you with healing and protective light. As you breathe out, visualize stress, tension, worry, and fear leaving your body. Continue to breathe in and out.

Slowly become aware of your head and neck. Feel your tension melting away and feel your head and neck begin to relax. Feel this relaxation slowly moving down through your shoulders as you continue to breathe in healing light and energy. Feel the relaxation move down into your arms and chest. Know that you are safe and you are loved.

Breathe in . . . and out. Breathe in . . . and out.

Feel the relaxation moving down into your waist and legs. Feel the tension and stress leaving your body. Feel the relaxation moving down into your feet. Feel your connection to the earth and the connection to your Higher Power.

As you continue to breathe deeply, imagine a place where you feel completely safe and serene. This may be the mountains, the beach, the forest. Wherever this place is, it is yours. Imagine yourself there right now. Take a look around and focus on what you see.

What do you smell? What do you hear?

Let all of your senses experience the serenity and safety of this special place. Know that this is your place that you can come to at any time.

Slowly begin to visualize how your Higher Power might look and feel. Let the image begin to fill your mind, body, and spirit.

Imagine your body and spirit being filled with serenity, contentment, and peace.

Feel your spirit connecting with your Higher Power. Feel the infinite wisdom and love your Higher Power has for you. Feel the safety and protection it offers you.

Know that your Higher Power guides your path in recovery and is with you at all times.

Know that you can connect with your Higher Power and your safe place any time you choose through prayer and meditation.

Know that you are not alone in your recovery. You are surrounded by love and support if you choose to let it in.

As you continue to breathe, gently become aware of your body. Become aware of your head . . . your neck . . . your shoulders and arms. Become aware of your back . . . your chest . . . your waist . . . your legs . . . your feet. Become aware of your connection to the earth. When you are ready, open your eyes.

Remember that the purpose of this imagery is to help you visualize and connect with your Higher Power. Each day through prayer and meditation you are able to feel this sense of connection and guidance from a Power greater than yourself. Spiritual fitness, like physical fitness, requires dedication.

Spiritual Pathway

Check any of the phrases that describe your spiritual pathway.

Singing/music   _____

Maintaining quiet, solitude   _____

Appreciating nature   _____

Loving others unselfishly   _____

Listening to others   _____

Sharing your feelings   _____

Keeping a journal   _____

Forgiving others   _____

Attending a church, synagogue, or other place of worship   _____

Praising others   _____

Smiling, laughing   _____

Reading, learning   _____

Helping others   _____

Sharing experiences   _____

Asking for forgiveness   _____

Embracing loved ones   _____

Twelve Steps Meditating   _____

Other spiritual practice   _____

Forgiveness

Family Objective

To ascertain the meaning of forgiveness.

Materials Needed

Handout – Forgiveness

Starting Point

The topic of forgiveness naturally occurs in the treatment process and when it does the following didactic will focus discussion. Facilitator needs to begin this session by asking family members their thoughts on forgiveness and then incorporating the didactic as appropriate.

Didactic

Families in early recovery or initial treatment often have mixed feelings regarding forgiveness. Some feel everything is forgivable, while others want to forgive from a position of false hope or perhaps they are not able to tolerate their painful feelings. People healing from family wounds become very confused about forgiveness, feeling there is a strong "should" attached to it, believing they "should" be able to forgive. This belief carries a message of good or bad and right or wrong. You are good if you forgive, bad if you do not. You are right if you forgive; you are wrong if you do not. Other messages are implied when family members believe they should forgive but don't feel ready to do it. One implication is that they are angry, thus they are bad people.

Whether or not you are able to forgive others is not the focus of treatment or recovery. Forgiveness is something you may ask for yourself; it is something you may be able to grant others. However, you may still be angry and hurt, and not ready to truly forgive. Forgiveness is not about being good or bad, right or wrong. It is about being true to yourself.

Only in knowing what forgiveness means to you can you put it into a healing perspective. The following thoughts may be helpful to you as you sort through your feelings and come to terms with the role forgiveness has in your healing. By recognizing what forgiveness is not, it is more possible to see what forgiveness is.

Give participants the handout *Forgiveness* and then continue.

What Forgiveness Is Not

Forgiveness is not forgetting.
You cannot forget what has happened, nor should you. Past experiences and the attendant pain have a great deal to teach you about not being victimized again and about not victimizing others.

Forgiveness is not condoning.
By forgiving the people who hurt you, you are not saying that what was done to you was acceptable, or unimportant, or "not so bad." It was important. It hurt, and it has made a difference in your life.

Forgiveness is not absolution.
Forgiving others does not absolve them; it doesn't "erase" what they have done. They are still responsible for the harm they caused.

Forgiveness is not a form of self-sacrifice.
In forgiving, you are not swallowing your true feelings; forgiving does not mean playing martyr. There is a real difference between repressing a feeling and releasing a feeling. Forgiveness doesn't mean you are never angry again about what occurred. What happened to you was hurtful. It was not right; it was not fair. For that you may always feel anger. You have every reason and right to be angry. But it's important to get to a point that your anger no longer interferes with how you care about yourself or how you live your life.

Forgiveness doesn't happen by making a one-time decision.
No matter how sincerely you want to let go of the past and move on with your life, you cannot just wave a magic wand and in one moment blithely make the past disappear. There is a process of grief work that you must walk through for forgiveness to occur.

What Forgiveness Is

Forgiveness is recognizing you no longer need your grudges and resentments, your hatred, your self-pity.
You do not need these negative emotions as excuses for getting less out of life than you want or deserve. You do not need them as weapons to hurt those who hurt you or to keep other people from getting close enough to hurt you again.

Forgiveness is no longer wanting to punish the people who hurt you.
Realizing that you truly do not want to "even the score," forgiveness is the inner peace you feel when you stop trying to do so.

Forgiveness is no longer building an identity around something that happened to you in the past.
You realize that there is more to you than your past. You put the past into its proper perspective as one dimension of who you are in the present.

Forgiveness is what happens naturally as a result of confronting past painful experiences and healing old wounds.

Forgiveness is an internal process; it happens within.

Forgiveness is a moral right, not a moral obligation. Forgiveness is remembering and letting go.

For most people, forgiveness is something you experience gradually over time. As the work of recovery and healing takes place, anger and hurt are often replaced by forgiveness and deeply felt spiritual acceptance. With every tear you shed and every cry of rage you release, more room is opened for forgiveness to enter your heart. As you do the work of healing, forgiveness manifests itself in your life by degrees. What is necessary for healing is a commitment to healing; forgiveness will then take care of itself.

Forgiveness

What Forgiveness Is Not

Forgiveness is not forgetting.

You cannot forget what has happened, nor should you. Past experiences and the attendant pain have a great deal to teach you about not being victimized again and about not victimizing others.

Forgiveness is not condoning.

By forgiving the people who hurt you, you are not saying that what was done to you was acceptable, or unimportant, or "not so bad." It was important. It hurt, and it has made a difference in your life.

Forgiveness is not absolution.

Forgiving others does not absolve them; it doesn't "erase" what they have done. They are still responsible for the harm they caused.

Forgiveness is not a form of self-sacrifice.

In forgiving, you are not swallowing your true feelings; forgiving does not mean playing martyr. There is a real difference between repressing a feeling and releasing a feeling.

Forgiveness doesn't mean you are never angry again about what occurred.

What happened to you was hurtful. It was not right; it was not fair. For that you may always feel anger. You have every reason and right to be angry. But it's important to get to a point that your anger no longer interferes with how you care about yourself or how you live your life.

Forgiveness doesn't happen by making a one-time decision.

No matter how sincerely you want to let go of the past and move on with your life, you cannot just wave a magic wand and in one moment blithely make the past disappear. There is a process of grief work that you must walk through for forgiveness to occur.

What Forgiveness Is

Forgiveness is recognizing you no longer need your grudges and resentments, your hatred, your self-pity.

You do not need these negative emotions as excuses for getting less out of life than you want or deserve. You do not need them as weapons to hurt those who hurt you or to keep other people from getting close enough to hurt you again.

Forgiveness is no longer wanting to punish the people who hurt you.

Realizing that you truly do not want to "even the score," forgiveness is the inner peace you feel when you stop trying to do so.

Forgiveness is no longer building an identity around something that happened to you in the past. You realize that there is more to you than your past. You put the past into its proper perspective as one dimension of who you are in the present.

Forgiveness is what happens naturally as a result of confronting past painful experiences and healing old wounds.

Forgiveness is an internal process; it happens within. Forgiveness is a moral right, not a moral obligation.

Forgiveness is remembering and letting go.

Assertive Rights

Family Objectives

To reinforce personal rights.

To establish a framework for healthy communication.

Materials Needed

Handout – Assertive Rights and Philosophy

Starting Point

This session could be spontaneously incorporated into the treatment process at the facilitator's discretion. A part of recovery is being able to hold oneself in esteem and honor one's personal rights. The handout *Assertive Rights and Philosophy* spells out a personal bill of rights and a basic philosophy in support of those rights. Review the handout with the participants. Ask them to identify the rights they want to be particularly vigilant to, then you can flush out the expressed right by having participants clarify behaviorally what it would look or sound like to follow through with a specific right.

For example:

What would it look like to express feelings?
A response might be: "I'd be more verbal. I'd let someone see my tears."

What would it sound like to change your mind?
A response might be: "I'd call up my friend and tell him I'd thought about 'such and such' and I've changed my mind."

What would it sound like to ask for what you want?
A response might be: "At first I would hear my own nervousness, but I would be able to say no and express what I want."

What would it look like to set your own priorities?
A response might be: "I'd see myself being more assertive, taking control, and I'd feel myself smiling inside."

You can work further with this by asking each participant to stand and verbalize a right repeatedly until they sound convincing. If working in a group, each participant can verbalize the right to the others in the group, or everyone on the group can join in at the same time by approaching other group members with their right. Listen for a convincing tone of expression and if helpful, challenge participants to be more assertive.

Assertive Rights and Philosophy

1. I have the right to express my feelings.

2. I have the right to be treated with respect.

3. I have the right to say no and not feel guilty.

4. I have the right to ask for information.

5. I have the right to make mistakes.

6. I have the right to change my mind.

7. I have the right to say, "I don't know."

8. I have the right to ask for what I want.

9. I have the right to set my own priorities.

10. I have the right to set boundaries to protect myself.

1. By standing up for myself, and letting myself be known to others, I gain self-respect from other people.

2. By trying to live in such a way that I never cause anyone to feel hurt under any circumstances, I end up hurting myself and other people.

3. Standing up for myself, and expressing my honest feelings and thoughts in a direct and appropriate way, is a winning process. Demeaning myself is a losing process.

4. By sacrificing my integrity and denying my personal feelings, relationships are damaged or prevented from developing. Likewise, personal relationships are damaged when I try to control others through hostility, intimidation, or guilt.

5. Personal relationships become more authentic and satisfying when I share my true reactions with others and don't block them from sharing their reactions with me.

6. Not letting others know what I think and feel is just as inconsiderate as not listening to other people's thoughts and feelings.

7. When I sacrifice my rights, I teach other people to take advantage of me.

8. By acting assertively and telling other people how their behavior affects me, I am giving them an opening to change their behavior. I am showing respect for their right to know where they stand with me.

Family Meetings

Family Objectives

To promote the art of listening.

To provide a safe place to share feelings without interruption or judgment.

Materials Needed

Handout – Family Meetings

Starting Point

Family meetings provide a structured format for coming together to promote the cohesiveness of the family. The format can be used with couples, larger family units, and families with children at home or of adult age. Introduce the concept and ascertain family members' thoughts about such a meeting. Because of variation in family units, the facilitator needs to assess the family in treatment and organize the logistics and focus of a family meeting. Holding a mock family meeting helps the family feel more confident in doing it on their own.

Didactic

Family meetings can be wonderful rituals. They facilitate opportunities for support and affirmation, healthy communication, family connection, and problem-solving. If such meetings are introduced in the process of gradual change in a newly recovering family they are more likely to be successful.

Most families who are still raising children choose to have a meeting weekly. It is always possible to have a nightly mini-version. If the children are independent and living away from home, it may be most practical to meet monthly. First and foremost, the frequency, time of day, and the location must be workable. While face-to-face meetings are best, families living at great distance from one another might place a conference call on the telephone or use instant messaging on the internet. A family meeting itself would be a great place to make these decisions with everyone's input.

A sacred time and place for family meetings needs to be agreed upon by all family members. Once a family agrees upon a realistic amount of time it is essential that the sacred time be honored above any other activity or event. Keeping a special time for the family meeting demonstrates the family members see the family as more important than anything else. Cell phones, television, radio, or any other electronic device need to be turned off. Any outside intrusion needs to be guarded against.

Ground rules help. Everyone gets a chance to talk; one person talks at a time without interruption. Everyone listens; only positive constructive feedback is allowed. Each meeting begins with a different person. If a child is resistant, you can offer incentives such as a post-meeting pizza or a special position, such as the rule enforcer, etc. You could also establish that any family member can call a family meeting to address a particular issue. Such meetings may be only minutes in length; nonetheless, the time is honored as "family meeting time." That means all family members come together to listen in the spirit of cooperation.

Suggested agendas for family meetings:
- *Feelings.* Everyone shares the feelings they have experienced this week. Feelings don't have to be specific to family relationships but they should be the predominant focus. If someone has feelings about something important to them outside of the family, it is still relevant that they see the family as a safe place in which to share, be heard, and supported. In a feelings meeting, the agenda is not to problem-solve feelings (unless the speaker asks for assistance in problem-solving); the goals are to share and be heard. If someone asks for assistance in problem-solving, continue through the group so everyone has the opportunity to share their feelings. Then go around a second time for problem-solving.

- *Family Business.* Everyone contributes to problem-solving issues concerning household tasks, such as who is feeding the pets, mowing the lawn, or money issues such as allowances, summer jobs, cars, and insurance. Family business might have to do with coping with a family stressor, such as the absence of a family member or one with an illness. Perhaps it will be a meeting for each person to present a situation for which they are open to input for problem-solving. It could be a current problem, or it could be a situation that occurred in the past week and even though it has already been taken care of, receiving input should it occur again would be helpful. It could be an individual problem outside the family or it might involve members of the family.

- *Family Rituals.* The idea of creating rituals, particularly around holiday or birthday celebrations, could be the topic of a family meeting. Healthy families keep traditions and form family rituals. Members of such families see themselves as part of a unit larger than themselves and they take pleasure in belonging. This is a great time to involve children in creating new rituals. Ask family members what types of family traditions they have liked and what they would like to incorporate into the family. Be creative, but take it slow and keep it simple. This is an opportunity for powerful family healing.

- *Affirmation.* In every meeting there is possibility for affirmation of self and others. You might begin each meeting by having family members share what they did this week that was good for them or that supported their recovery. A young child might say, "I asked a question in class," when in the past he or she would have wondered about something and not asked. A teenager might say, "I didn't go out with a group of kids that I knew were going to get into some trouble," or, "I called home and asked to be picked up when I was with some friends and they started to smoke dope." A mother might say, "I let you cry without trying to stop you," when in the past she would have tried to convince her daughter she didn't need to feel bad. A father might say, "I am making a point to leave work early so that I get home in time for dinner."

A fun way to conclude a family meeting is with affirmations of self. Family members say something positive about themselves and once they say it, the family cites back, "Yes you are!"

"I am a fun person to be with."	"Yes you are!"
"I am a loving person."	"Yes you are!"
"I am worthy."	"Yes you are!"

Family Meetings

A sacred time and place for family meetings needs to be agreed upon by all family members. Once a family agrees upon a realistic amount of time it is essential that the sacred time be honored above any other activity or event. Keeping a special time for the family meeting demonstrates that family members see the family as more important than anything else. Cell phones, the television, radio, pagers, etc., need to be turned off. Any outside intrusion needs to be guarded against.

Ground rules help. Everyone gets a chance to talk; one person talks at a time without interruption. Everyone listens; only positive constructive feedback is allowed. Each meeting begins with a different person. If a child is resistant, you can offer incentives such as a post-meeting pizza or a special position, such as the rule enforcer, etc. You could also establish that any family member can call a family meeting to address a particular issue. Such meetings may be only minutes in length; nonetheless, the time is honored as "family meeting time." That means all family members come together to listen in the spirit of cooperation.

Suggested agendas for family meetings:

- *Feelings.* Everyone shares the feelings they have experienced this week. Feelings don't have to be specific to family relationships but they should be the predominant focus. If someone has feelings about something important to them outside of the family, it is still relevant that they see the family as a safe place in which to share, be heard, and supported. In a feelings meeting, the agenda is not to problem-solve feelings (unless the speaker asks for assistance in problem-solving); the goals are to share and be heard. If someone asks for assistance in problem-solving, continue through the group so everyone has the opportunity to share their feelings. Then go around a second time for problem-solving.
- *Family Business.* Everyone contributes to problem-solving issues concerning household tasks, such as who is feeding the pets, mowing the lawn, or money issues such as allowances, summer jobs, cars, and insurance. Family business might have to do with coping with a family stressor, such as the absence of a family member or one with an illness. Perhaps it will be a meeting for each person to present a situation for which they are open to input for problem-solving. It could be a current problem, or it could be a situation that occurred in the past week and even though it has already been taken care of, receiving input should it occur again would be helpful. It could be an individual problem outside the family or it might involve members of the family.
- *Family Rituals.* The idea of creating rituals, particularly around holiday or birthday celebrations, could be the topic of a family meeting. Healthy families keep traditions and form family rituals. Members of such families see themselves as part of a unit larger than themselves and they take pleasure in belonging. This is a great time to involve children in creating new rituals. Ask family members what types of family traditions they have liked and what they would like to incorporate into the family. Be creative but take it slow and keep it simple. This is an opportunity for powerful family healing.

- *Affirmation.* In every meeting there is possibility for affirmation of self and others. You might begin each meeting by having family members share what they did this week that was good for them or that supported their recovery. A young child might say, "I asked a question in class," when in the past he or she would have wondered about something and not asked. A teenager might say, "I didn't go out with a group of kids that I knew were going to get into some trouble," or, "I called home and asked to be picked up when I was with some friends and they started to smoke dope." A mother might say, "I let you cry without trying to stop you," when in the past she would have tried to convince her daughter she didn't need to feel bad. A father might say, "I am making a point to leave work early so that I can get home in time for dinner."

A fun way to conclude a family meeting is with affirmations of self. Family members say something positive about themselves and once they say it, the family cites back, "Yes you are!"

"I am a fun person to be with."	"Yes you are!"
"I am a loving person."	"Yes you are!"
"I am worthy."	"Yes you are!"

Portrait of Recovery

Family Objective

To identify specific behaviors that demonstrate healing and recovery.

Materials Needed

Handout – Recovery Questions

Starting Point

This session is held to give family members an opportunity to create a vision or portrait of recovery, to identify codependent behaviors, and to be specific about what recovery means. Creating this vision of recovery helps them to solidify recovery behaviors. The *Recovery Questions* handout is most effective when offered as an assignment so that ample time is available for serious reflection. The assignment could also be given as an art/collage exercise.

When participants are able to be specific with their answers to questions two, three, and four, then they have identifiable goals. The more specific they can be about their recovery practices in question five (Twelve Step meetings, the use of sponsors, daily meditations, readings, etc.), the greater the likelihood they will experience recovery. If they are unable to identify recovery practices, it is unlikely they will achieve their goals.

This exercise is ideal to use to close a brief therapy program. It may also be used in the middle of a lengthier therapy program (six months or more) as it reinforces the recovery process.

Recovery Questions

1. What does your codependency look like presently, and in the past?

2. What does your personal recovery look like?

3. What do you see yourself doing differently?

4. How would someone recognize it?

5. What practices support your recovery?

Recovery Plan

Family Objective

To create a recovery self-care plan.

Materials Needed

Handout – My Recovery Plan

Starting Point

Addicted people in treatment are encouraged to develop a relapse prevention plan. Family members pursuing recovery need to develop a plan as well. Prior to participants developing a recovery plan, dialogue with them about:

1. Behaviors they want to change.
2. What they will do to facilitate and support changes.
3. Behaviors they want to keep.
4. What they will do to support behaviors they will keep.
5. What resources they will use.
   - Twelve Step programs
   - Therapy
   - Friends
   - Church
   - Yoga/Exercise
   - Other
   - Meditation
   - Journaling

A recovery plan is quite personal, so it needs to be specific to each family member. An innovative model of a recovery plan uses the analogy of streetlights—red light, yellow light, and green light behaviors. Share the following information before having participants complete their recovery plans.

Didactic

Red Light Behaviors

Behaviors that need to be stopped. These are behaviors that are destructive to yourself and to others. Examples: verbal rage, driving while angry or in tears, waiting up all night for the addicted person to come home.

Yellow Light Behaviors

Behaviors that require caution. These are behaviors, people, places and/or things that trigger self-destructive or uncaring acts toward self and that jeopardize recovery. Pulling the trigger on a gun signals that a bullet is about to be fired. For family members, triggers are behaviors and situations that can easily lead back into enabling or codependent behaviors. Examples: listening to the addicted person explain why you should loan him or her money; being in a social situation with people who have been part of the addicted person's acting out behavior; or while traveling you call home and no one answers. It is important to learn to assess for potential high-risk situations and triggers to unhealthy behavior. Triggers differ for each family member.

This means knowing what triggers your yellow light behavior. One particularly strong trigger is euphoric recall. This is when past experiences or situations are romanticized and the negative consequences are forgotten. Social stressors present significant triggers. When you start to feel pressured and uncomfortable, the urge to return to codependent behavior can feel overwhelming.

Green Light Behaviors

Behaviors to take care of yourself. These can be spiritual, physical, emotional, intellectual, and/or sexual behaviors that characterize and support the recovery process. Examples: spiritual—read daily meditations in the morning; physical—eat breakfast, take a walk after work; emotional—make an emotional check-in with self two times a day; intellectual—ask a question when it's not clear what someone means; sexual—let your partner know when you want to be sexually intimate. One area that you may find particularly difficult is the amount of extra time you have in recovery. Often you spent hours or days each week engaging in preoccupation with the addicted person and his or her behavior. Now in recovery, it feels as though there is a void. It is important to identify and engage in positive activities to account for the extra time.

When family members begin a recovery self-care plan, it is usually easier for them to identify red or green light behaviors. Yellow light behaviors often necessitate more in-depth thought and discussion. If there are apparent behaviors a family member hasn't identified, the facilitator may make suggestions. But be cautious; you are not looking for compliance but for them to create a self-care plan that they would be willing to commit to. The more specific the behaviors and intentions the greater the likelihood they can follow through.

Depending on the length of time family members are in therapy, this plan can be reevaluated and changed at any time during or after the treatment process. Give participants the handout *My Recovery Plan* as an assignment so that they can work on it without time restriction.

Recovery plan adapted from a model by Diane Dillon

My Recovery Plan

 Red Light Behaviors

Behaviors I need to change:

1. _____

_____

2. _____

_____

3. _____

_____

4. _____

_____

How I can accomplish this change:

1. _____

_____

2. _____

_____

3. _____

_____

4. _____

_____

What might interfere with changing my red light behaviors?

_____

_____

_____

 Yellow Light Behaviors

Behaviors and/or situations I need to be cautious of:

1. _____

_____

2. _____

_____

3. _____

_____

4. _____

_____

What I can do to prevent them:

1. _____

_____

2. _____

_____

3. _____

_____

4. _____

_____

What might interfere with my awareness of yellow light behaviors/situations?

_____

_____

_____

Who can I talk to if I find myself "running a yellow light?"

1. _____

2. _____

3. _____

Green Light Behaviors

What I need to do to take care of myself:

1. _____

_____

2. _____

_____

3. _____

_____

4. _____

_____

How I can accomplish this:

1. _____

_____

2. _____

_____

3. _____

_____

4. _____

_____

What might interfere with my green light behaviors?

_____

_____

_____

On this day (fill in date)_____,I make a commitment to myself to stop my red light behaviors, be cautious and aware of my yellow light behaviors, and follow through on my green light behaviors.

_____
(signature)

Closing Ritual

Family Objective

To experience a healthy closure.

Materials Needed

Optional: Certificate, coin, or another symbol of treatment completion

Starting Point

For addictive families, both beginnings and endings are usually troublesome. A healthy closing to the family treatment process is important whether the facilitator is working in private practice with one family member, a couple or entire family, or working in a time-limited family addiction program. If the facilitator does not have a final closing ritual, the following exercises can be utilized.

Closing Ritual:

- In a circle, as each participant takes a turn, the other participants share, one by one, an affirmation with them. Examples are:
  What I really value about you is—
  What I have most appreciated about you is—
- Present a tangible object such as a certificate, coin, or another symbol of their completion and moving on as an affirmation of their commitment to their recovery process.
- Offer an imagery of affirmation and closure to the family members' experiences in these sessions.

Imagery Direction

When asking people to participate in an imagery, begin by acknowledging that it may feel awkward in the beginning, but that it can be highly valuable if they allow themselves to relax and be open to the process.

It is suggested that you have soft music playing in the background. The key is for the presenter to talk slowly, and allow the participants time to breathe deeply, to hear the words, to be with the words. It is not necessary to have a discussion about the imagery once completed. In fact, that is often contraindicated because it moves the participant from an emotional/spiritual experience into an intellectual realm.

Begin the experience by asking the participants to find a comfortable sitting position, uncross their arms and legs, and begin to take slow deep breaths in and out. As you offer these directions, begin to pace your speaking so that it is soothing and relaxing.

Closure Imagery

Slowly breathe in . . . and out. Breathe in . . . and out.

As you breathe in, imagine healing energy beginning to move throughout your body. Allow the muscles in your face, neck, and shoulders to soften and relax. Breathe in calming energy . . . breathe out tension. Feel this calm and healing energy move down through your chest and arms into your waist and legs. Feel your stress and tension melt away. Feel your connection to your Higher Power. Know that you are safe in this room and you are loved.

Begin to visualize all of the tools you have gathered to strengthen your recovery. You have tools to focus on relationships, powerlessness, control, shame, secrets, anger, feelings, and many other aspects of your life that are important in recovery. Today, you will focus on many of these tools and remember that you have done a great deal of work to strengthen your recovery and prevent relapse. You are never immune to relapse, but if you choose to use your tools each day, your recovery is strengthened.

You have tools to help you focus on healthy, nurturing relationships.

Say to yourself:
    I deserve to have a healthy and nurturing relationship with myself.

You have tools for letting go of control.

Say to yourself:

> *Today, I choose to let go of my resentments and control.*
> *Today, acceptance is the answer to all my problems.*
> *Today, I will let my Higher Power guide my journey.*

You have tools for releasing shame and secrets.

Say to yourself:

> *Today, I choose to release shame messages I have received from others and shame I have about myself.*
> *I choose to surround myself with healthy people in my recovery.*
> *Today, I choose to live my life in honesty and recovery.*

You have tools for releasing anger.

Say to yourself:

> *Today, I choose to release my anger.*
> *I choose to live my life filled with serenity and peace.*
> *I choose to surround myself with people who are serene and peaceful.*

You have tools for your grief and other feelings.

Say to yourself:

> *Today, I know that I am safe to have feelings and I can choose to express my feelings.*
> *Today, I choose to surround myself with people who are safe to express my feelings with.*

You have tools for when you may experience warning signs and triggers.

Say to yourself:

> *I may experience warning signs and triggers.*
> *If I do, I will immediately use my relapse plan and ask others for help.*
> *I am not alone in my recovery.*
> *People who love me and support my recovery surround me in my recovery program.*
> *I am not alone.*

Today, my program of recovery is the most important thing in my life.
If I make anything or anyone else more important than my program, I may have a relapse.
Today, I have the tools to nourish my spiritual program of recovery.

Remember, these tools work only when you use them. Each day in recovery, it is important to use these tools wisely.

Say to yourself:
   I am precious.
   I am worthy of recovery.
   I love myself.
   I am able to receive love and support from others.

As you continue to breathe deeply, slowly and gently become aware of your body in this room. Become aware of your head . . . your neck . . . your shoulders and arms. Become aware of your back . . . your chest . . . your waist . . . your legs . . . your feet. Become aware of your connection to the earth. Gently begin to shift your body around and when you are ready, open your eyes.

Closing Thoughts

Dear Facilitator,

In all the years I have worked with families impacted by addiction my experience continues to be one of incredible gratitude. It is an honor for me to witness the courage family members demonstrate in looking within themselves, meeting their resistances, changing life-long behaviors, and embarking on new paths of recovery. We are part of their recovery journey as guides, mentors, and facilitators. I thank them for allowing me to be a part of their treatment process and I applaud and thank you for the professional commitment you show to these families. No one deserves to live with the fear, confusion, and the pain that go along with addiction in the family. There is a path out.

Claudia Black